My Name is Aron

Journey to the light of freedom

As told to
S. J. Helgesen

DEDICATION

This book is dedicated to the millions of innocent souls who suffered persecution, humiliation, indescribable pain and ultimately death during the terrible nightmare of the Holocaust. It is also dedicated to all who continue to suffer at the hands of evil people that would ignore their own humanity simply to achieve dominion over others.

I dedicate my story to my dear mother and father who are in my daily thoughts and prayers these many years later. I thank them for raising me to be forgiving and tolerant and to be strong enough to fight to preserve the dignity and respect of all human beings. To my sweet brother, Filip, a soul whose time on earth went too swiftly, I say, "Shalom, Shalom," and to my twin sister go my thanks for her unconditional love for me. Finally, I dedicate this book to *hope*, the one thing all people need to survive.

ACKNOWLEDGMENTS

The idea of this book lay smoldering in the back of my mind for many years. The memories of the good times of my youth and those of my captivity have been competing with one another for my time ever since my liberation in 1945. Every once in awhile I would unburden myself to a journalist or interviewer, but then I would put the 'genie' back in the bottle and suppress the memories. That was until I met the Honorary German Consul in New Mexico, Stephan Helgesen, a man of talent and persuasiveness and one I am now proud to call my good friend. His interest in my story and his insistence that it be told is why you are now reading this, and I thank him sincerely for his efforts to help me re-construct those nearly five years of imprisonment.

I must also thank my teachers for keeping the flame of imagination burning bright within me; for showing me the value of a good education; and for teaching me about the power of words. My dear wife, Miriam, has been a constant source of inspiration and support throughout the writing of this book, and to her I express my sincere thanks. I am convinced that we are all more than the sum of our individual parts and more than the sum of the parts that others play in our lives. Like chapters in a book, each part can stand on its own but is stronger when connected to the others. My long life, each part of it, has truly been a gift from God, and to Him I owe everything.

Forward

*"Even the lowliest insect struggles to survive,
not because he knows why but because he knows he must."*

Mine is a small story, insignificant on its own, a simple thread. However, when combined with the millions of other stories from those who have shared my experiences, it has perhaps some value as part of a larger tapestry that will one day, God willing, be understood. With time, maybe it can quietly recede to the high bookshelf that is reserved for all the books filled with all the stories of all the lessons we've learned.

I am not the first, nor will I be the last to be persecuted for doing nothing wrong or for saying nothing wrong. Given man's history on this troubled planet, there will, unfortunately, be others whose only crime against society is their mere existence.

So it is with certain peoples, certain beliefs, and certain times. One still has hope, that by telling the stories of those who have suffered for these things, we will gain wisdom to appreciate the things that we have in common and learn tolerance for the things that serve to separate us.

The Holocaust really happened. I am a living witness. The senseless brutality and willful rendering of pain and torture on millions of innocent men, women and children, people of all faiths and backgrounds, really happened. In the twilight following those tumultuous years of savagery, something else also happened...the victims began to forgive.

For the spiritually barren and for the physically injured, forgiveness is always the first step that must be taken before a life of true meaning and purpose can be rebuilt. Yes, forgiveness is critical to rebuilding life.

Those who ignore it and would rather spend their days wrapped in a cocoon of hatred and recrimination are doomed to a life that will never truly be complete.

With God's help and with the help of many kind and decent people, my life was spared. I continue to spend my days wondering why, but know in my heart that the best way to pay them all back is to live life well.

Aron Straser

CONTENTS

CHAPTER 1

Life in Smorgon

The year was 1925 when my twin sister Rachel and I came into this world, born to a family of little means in the small town of Smorgon, or Smorgonie as we called it, in eastern Poland. It lay almost mid-way between the Lithuanian city of Vilnius (Vilno) and the Russian city of Minsk.

It was six years after the bloody European war known as *the Great War or the war to end all wars*, World War I, a war that claimed the lives of 16 million people. While Europe was breathing a sigh of relief that the enormous death and destruction from that war was past and the job of rebuilding had begun, war once again erupted in Poland in 1920.

The new Soviet Union flexed its muscles on my native Poland which had just gained its independence after 123 years of partitioning. Fortunately for Poland, the war ended almost as quickly as it had begun with its borders re-drawn once again.

Though an extremely important situation for my country's leaders, it was an issue of no importance five years later to an infant taking his first breaths and crying for his breakfast. From a practical standpoint, it also meant little to my parents whose interest in world politics was overshadowed by the need to stay warm and feed their now five-person family. Such is the pattern of daily life when one is an ordinary worker with no power to change the course of events beyond one's own doorstep.

Smorgonie was a town of 10,000. About 40% of the population was Jewish as was my family. We lived among non-Jewish neighbors in the village. Large and small farms encircled us, many of which were rented out by the wealthy landowners.

To me, Smorgonie was a place of wonderment as young child. Though we lived in town, we were never far from a vast playground of trees and forest, meadows and dales and a river to swim in. The climate was far from balmy.

Winters were often very harsh with plenty of snow and freezing temperatures.

Springs were filled with the sounds of birds and blossoming wildflowers. Summers were blessed with the sun and the beautiful Falls were laced with the unmistakable crispness of fresh air. Like the children in hundreds of other towns, we played at every opportunity. The adults worked endlessly.

The challenge of making ends meet, financially, was always present but mostly belonged to my parents. As a young boy, my thoughts were focused on any mystery of nature I could unlock. My eyes alternated from gazing up at the vast expanse of sky to watching the events of life that unfolded on our streets.

This was my daily routine along with performing the many chores given to me by my mother, Rivka, a wonderfully caring woman born at the turn of the century in Smorgonie. She married my father during the war and changed her name from Lapidus to his, Struczanski (I later Americanized it to Straser).

I remember her as being a very clever woman who could take a simple piece of cloth and turn it into a thing of pure beauty. She was also musically talented and had a wonderful singing voice that could hold a high note but also be very stern when necessary to scold us for our mischief.

My father, Jona, who was four years older than my mother, was a strong hard-working man who was proud of his family and was dedicated to providing for them. My older brother, Filip, was six years older than me. He was a quiet sort of person, very kind and very protective of my sister and myself. As the oldest, he was often called upon to do the 'heavy lifting' chores but always without a complaint passing his lips. I looked up to him and loved him, though saying, "I love you" then was not as common an occurrence as it is today.

My twin sister, Rachel, was quiet in her own sort of way, a happy child but cautious. Her play was less adventurous than mine and she clung like most girls to our mother who taught her the things that girls needed to learn back then: cooking and sewing. We all lived in a two family house (my aunt and uncle and their two sons lived in the front and we lived in the back) on a street called Ulica Krewska.

There was a synagogue on our street and Ulica Krewska was populated mostly by Jewish families. When I grew to school age I attended the local public school, but I also attended the Jewish school.

When I grew old enough to play *Laptu*, a form of baseball, I played with many boys. Some were Jews and some not. I felt no discrimination on the ball field or anywhere else for that matter. We were just boys, without religious or class differences, just youngsters having fun. We knew nothing of politics or of armed conflicts going on outside our country.

Though we were close to Russia (the new Soviet Union) we spoke only Polish outside the home. Inside and at the synagogue we spoke Yiddish (and for our Talmud studies, Hebrew). Our world was small, small enough to be insulated from the forces that were growing in the new Nazi Germany or the Bolshevik Soviet Union.

The first dozen years of my life were blissfully ignorant of such things. My focus was on fun and frolic, friendly competition and camaraderie.

Our home was like many of the day, sparse, without luxury of any kind. We heated with a stove in a central room, pumped water from a well outside and of course took care of the 'necessities' in an outhouse separate from the main house. We had no radio because they were expensive and because we had no electricity.

Candles and kerosene lamps were our only illumination. I can still recall the pungent smell of the kerosene and remember the dirt it left behind on our clothes.

Our food was purchased locally: vegetables, potatoes and other roots bought from the local market and which were supplied by the surrounding farms. Meat was expensive and a treat when we could get it. We made do as best we could, and my mother was a wizard with a cooking pot, trying her best to be creative with whatever she had in the larder.

I was an energetic student if not an excellent one. Learning geography and history were like a big story-telling session to me. I don't remember ever longing to travel, but I do remember traveling in my thoughts to exotic places (anyplace outside Smorgonie was exotic!).

I was a good student of the Talmud, however. Hebrew school was very different from our public school. I was part of a greater whole there, comfortable within a group of people who shared a common heritage and history.

Not that I thought of myself in terms of Jewish first, Polish second. Being Jewish just added a dimension that rounded out my own personal background and I liked that. Maybe I felt a bit special but certainly not better than my non-Jewish friends.

The Jews of Poland had a protector in the Polish government, a man who helped hold the forces of prejudice that bubbled up every once in a while in check. He was General Jozef Pilsudski and he was the person most responsible for the creation of the second republic of Poland in 1918 (123 years after it had been taken over by Russia, Austria and Prussia).

To many Polish Jews he was a hero who believed in a multicultural society that recognized the many ethnic and religious groups like ours.

He was the Head of State in Poland for a brief four years, right before and nearly three and a half years after the end of WWI. In 1920, he commanded Polish forces in six border wars and even vanquished the Russian army in the Battle of Warsaw in August of that year.

After withdrawing from politics in 1923 he came back, as a benign dictator, in a coup in 1926 and led Poland – never once allowing anti-Jewish laws to become the law of the land.

To my parents and to those of us who knew of his exploits, he was a hero of the first order. Little did we know that when he died in 1935, when I was just ten years old, that his protection of us would die with him.

The field was then left to politicians who were not as enamored of the Polish Jewish population that had turned out in droves to support Pilsudski. Within a few short years after his departure, Poland's sovereignty and our small world in Smorgonie would be turned upside down.

My earliest memories were of my father and mother working with cloth, in a kind of haberdashery business. This business gave my sister and me the opportunity to 'see the world' outside of Smorgonie. My parents would load up a borrowed horse-drawn farmer's wagon with bolts of cloth and travel all through the night to the neighboring villages of Solly or Krevo to sell their wares.

The nighttime ride was magical and maybe a bit scary for a little boy like me, but I savored the adventure. The weather didn't always cooperate, and when the rain came we all crowded together under a huge waterproof cover that kept us dry. The odor of the cloth, the moist air outside, the trees and grass along the narrow path (plus the horse) combined to form a rich palette of sights and smells I'll never forget.

The next day, we would set up, along with many other vendors, in a large meadow, a place that had a kind of Middle Eastern bazaar atmosphere to it what with all the bustle and sounds of people hawking their wares. These were big markets where they would sell everything: animals, milk, dry goods, food, etc. It was an exchange, and everybody had something to sell.

Every person needed something. Customers would seek us out to buy our cloth. Ours was not a tailoring business; we just sold cloth. We children helped out to make sure nothing went 'missing' from the stock when my father's or mother's backs were turned. If someone was acting suspiciously we would talk to our parents in Yiddish so the people who were the object of our discussion wouldn't understand.

I remember once there was a very big lady wearing a very big overcoat, and it seemed to me that she would open it up once in a while and put something in it and then close it quickly. I quietly alerted my father to her who promptly went up to her and in his deliberate but friendly voice said, "Did you forget to pay?" Flustered, she said, "Oh, I'm sorry. How much was that now?"

These outings at the villages were also a proving ground for a young pup like me. I am one hour older than my twin sister Rachel, and I was always trying to prove to her that I was faster or stronger or smarter or more clever. I wouldn't let her forget about the 'age difference' between us. After enduring enough of my teasing she would invariably storm away from me and turn to mother or father crying. I was a real 'Dennis the Menace' type as a child, at least as far as my sister is concerned.

My older brother, Filip, who was nearly five years older than me palled around with just a few boys his own age. His group wouldn't accept young, hangers-on like me or my friends. Their circle was impenetrable. Filip was a rather quiet type of person, not aggressive in any way.

He loved my mother and tended to be around her more than father. I think she felt sorry for him that he didn't have all that many friends.

Filip loved the excursions to the villages, and it was something we had in common. Sometimes our parents were away starting Sunday night and didn't come home until Wednesday. Filip would stand in for them, watching Rachel and me.

This life on the road was double duty for my mother as it is for any mother who works out of the house...they have to work inside the house when they come home. Things mounted up when one was away. There was always sewing, cooking and cleaning that needed to be done. And while we did our best to do our chores, I am sure we added more to my mother's workload than relieved it.

I wore 'open-seamed' clothing, hand-me-downs from my brother. Mother would open the seams and turn them inside out because the inside was fresher and showed less wear.

My mother was a genius at making suits for me and it was a good thing that I had no younger brother as we had run out of seams to turn inside out! When the holidays came, I would be trotted out in my finery, and I must say that my pride nearly burst my buttons, so good did I look. Even though my father also worked at a tannery we couldn't afford to buy any of the expensive hides so we never had any leather clothes, just leather shoes. The shoes were, of course, made to order because every kid needed a different size. No mass production with no stock on the shelves. It wasn't practical, but that's the way it was.

In my school, which was a public school, they tried to keep us separated by age. This was not the one-room schoolhouse of the American West. The Hebrew School was a private school and required tuition. Not everybody could afford it.

I was lucky enough to attend in the afternoons. There were about 4-5 grades. In addition to the Hebrew School, there were several synagogues in Smorgonie to accommodate the 40% of the population that was Jewish.

I loved geography and history. These were 'magic carpet' subjects that could transport you to other places and other times. I was also fond of arithmetic. I remember when I was in the fourth grade the teachers pulled me out and brought me over to the 5th or 6th grade room and put me up at the blackboard.

They gave me some problems to do which I did, quickly and correctly. I think I did well because I was praised by the teachers. Unfortunately, the other kids hated me for it.

My parents were very supportive of me in the school. My mother, herself, was a teacher. She taught the Russian language. She had a tremendous memory. Even at the age of 90 when she was living in the Boston area with my sister, her favorite thing was for Rachel and me to sit down while she recited a poem.

This was no short five-liner. It was a 15-minute poem in Russian no less! She had a brilliant and quick mind right up to the very end of her life.

My father's memory was also good, and he could remember many prayers in Hebrew. He was not blessed with a good singing voice, though. That was my mother's gift. My father was shy and he loved the out-of-doors. We all did.

I loved the summertime best of all. We often swam in the Vileya River. It was close to a grain mill that was owned by the father of one of my friends. I remember, vividly, a little waterfall of water spilling over the rocks to power the mill. It was something right off a postcard.

One time I followed the other youngsters into the river (I didn't know how to swim) and went in a little too far and tried to touch the bottom of the river bed but couldn't so I went under and gulped a few mouthfuls of water and started yelling for help.

They came to my aid and pulled me out but I begged them not to tell my parents because I feared that if they found out they would forbid me from ever going there again.

I am sure that German and Russian children were swimming in their own rivers just like me. Children are children and summers are summers.

We also had relatives outside Smorgonie, relatives on both sides of my family, but we were seldom in contact with them. Communication was bad and we only had a bicycle so there was no way, really, to keep in touch. Much later, when I moved to the U.S., I was able to re-connect with relatives and we managed to see each other for some of the high holy days.

Life in Smorgonie was nothing like the big cities of Vilnius or Minsk, but an occasional celebrity did come our way. There was a very famous cantor by the name of Moshe Koussevitzky. He was born in our village and had a fantastic voice. An American visitor once came to our village and was overwhelmed by his talent, and said he would send him to a cantorial school in Vilnius so he could learn to sing properly!

Koussevitzky moved to Vilna and went from being our cantor to becoming the main cantor at the largest synagogue there. Later, when the Russians entered into our part of Poland they took him back to Moscow with them to become a part of their opera company.

However, he was restricted from chanting any religious music. He could chant ordinary music like traditional folk music but not religious music.

Now here's my story about Koussevitsky. In 1940, we heard that he was coming to Smorgon. Everybody, I mean literally everybody in the Jewish community, wanted to see him. He was good friends with my uncle Maier who had worked with him in the same shoe shop when they were youngsters, but that's not the important part. I just tell you so that you know that we felt like we had a personal connection to him and this visit.

The buzz about Koussevitsky started long before the actual visit, so everyone, Jew and Gentile alike, was in a perpetual state of excitement, so huge was his talent and so wide was his fame. When the big day of his open air performance came he was accompanied by two Russian guards that monitored his every move.

As luck would have it, the two Russian guards had started to drink early (and much), and just before he was about to sing his state-approved medley of 'safe' non-religious music, the guards fell into a drunken sleep. Some would say that God had intervened. Others would blame the vodka.

Either way, two Russian guards were now so stiff and lifeless and unaware of what was going on around them that Koussevitsky was free to sing his music of choice.

I would be lying if I didn't say that we were all concerned that maybe the surrounding towns' police would hear about this departure from the program. After all, this was a huge event with about 4,000 people gathered in this area. Someone would surely say something! Fortunately, I was wrong. Nobody said anything. People knew that to tell tales would have meant the end of Moshe Koussevitsky's career and maybe even his life.

The secret of his deviation from the script never reached the Kremlin. We who were there will never forget it and the two Russian guards will never remember it. Some things are as they should be.

In 1937, things started to change after the passing of the 'Jewish protector' Marshall Pilsudski two years earlier. The two new racial laws of Nuremburg were already in force after being passed in 1935 at the Nazi Party congress. A man we'd never heard of, Adolf Hitler, was now in control of the reins of power in Germany. We knew that bad times were on the way.

Ill winds were blowing from the West and soon we would be in the center of a tornado that would carry us all away.

CHAPTER 2

Poland before the Nazis

In 1937, my world, the world of a 12-year old boy entering what should have been the wonder and excitement of his teenage years, was still-born as word of the Nazi hate machine and Germany's munitions build-up reached us.

The Nuremburg Laws, which basically institutionalized many of the racial theories prevalent in Nazi ideology excluded German Jews from Reich citizenship and prohibited them from marrying or having sexual relations with persons of "German or related blood." Other ordinances disenfranchised Jews and stripped them of their political rights.

The Laws did not define a "Jew" as someone with particular religious beliefs, but anyone who had three or four Jewish grandparents was defined as a Jew, regardless of whether that individual identified himself or herself as a Jew or belonged to the Jewish religious community.

We heard that many Germans who had not even practiced Judaism for years found themselves snared in the grip of Nazi terror. Even people with Jewish grandparents who had converted to Christianity were defined as Jews! Germany was fast closing its grip on Poland, and we feared that soon, the Nuremberg Laws would strangle our people, too.

In the spring of 1941, while we were under Russian rule (this was after the Russians annexed our region in 1939), 100 German-Jewish refugees ended up in our area. They all had Polish ancestry. They were driven out of Germany right away and taken to the border of Poland when the Germans decided to attack the Russian forces. After one short week of fighting they took over Poland. The Polish army collapsed and was in retreat.

My father knew probably better than the rest of us what horrors were on the way because of his two-year long incarceration as a prisoner in the First World War. (After his release he walked all the way home to Smorgonie).

I'm not sure where in Germany he was imprisoned, but according to him, "being a prisoner in Germany was no different than being a prisoner in any other country." Work was hard, but at least his life was spared.

I am now 15 years old and the tension of the times has totally replaced any of my childhood desires for leisure activity or horseplay. It is Sunday, the 22nd of June in 1941. While my non-Jewish friends are in church we were informed on our radio that the Germans were attacking us, and from the German-Jewish refugees we heard more stories of Jewish mistreatment.

The stories seemed so surreal to us. Jews in other small towns in Poland may have been subject to occasional harassment but nothing like the stories of persecution we heard from these refugees. That very day the refugees left for Lithuania or Latvia and perhaps from there had hoped to escape to Finland, Sweden or even Denmark. Suddenly they were gone and we were left with nothing but the echoes of their tales, though one couple did stay on for about a week.

These two knew Hebrew very well, and it was because of that they were hired as teachers in the Hebrew School. I remember them as being young, maybe in their 20s. At the end of the week they just disappeared. Everybody went to look for them because all their clothes and belongings were still in the small room they had rented. We found them at the bottom of a 15-foot well.

They decided that they couldn't face a life of persecution. We knew then that the refugees had not been lying to us.

I remember my parents were agonizing over what to do. The Russian border was maybe 75-100 miles away and we had no transportation except for my brother's bicycle, so we loaded it up with clothing and other things. It was so heavy that we could hardly move it.

Many of my brother's friends decided to just take off on their bicycles, leaving their families behind. My brother Filip insisted that he should stay behind. He felt that the rest of us should go. That was not meant to be, as my parents insisted that we would all go or none of us would go.

We eventually left and faced the long five-day journey to the Russian border. We all carried something and pushed Filip's bicycle. So heavily laden was it that you could not see where the tires left off and the ground began.

Our entire bodies were sore, especially our feet. For fear of running into 'unfriendlies' we tried to stick to the farm roads, not the main roads. Unfortunately, there were not many farmhouses along the way where we could overnight. After a few days we made it to the border to a city named Gorodok and found some Jews there in the village. They told us that we could not go any further because we were not Russian and we were Jewish.

The border guards were afraid too. They were afraid of spies crossing the border. We stayed in Gorodok, out in the open after unpacking the few blankets we had. Rumors abounded. I heard that somebody saw two farmers on horseback that had come to the village and were telling the people that the Germans were coming from the East.

Indeed, the German army had encircled a huge territory of Belarus, north and south, and had captured Minsk and they were 'mopping up' the area. They were moving back westward and had thousands of prisoners of war with them.

We saw them passing, but we were not allowed to communicate with them. They kept us away from them. We stayed where we were because we couldn't cross the border. They threatened to shoot us if we crossed. We were maybe a thousand people there at the border, just waiting.

They told us that we had to go back to where we came from so that we could get food rationing cards. We hoped that perhaps we could buy our way across the border by bribing the guards, but we couldn't. We stayed because we hoped that things would change.

The very same day that the farmers told us the Germans were coming, a few hours later, they showed up. When I saw the German army, first the tanks, the artillery and the heavy equipment and the trucks I remember thinking, "There was no end to it!"

The Polish police told us, "Clear the road. Move away." They had come with the Germans and saw us sitting on the ground. The first Germans that came on motorcycles flew the German flag and their military flag. They had translators, the Polish police, to speak with us.

The Polish police surrounded all thousand of us and separated the women from the men, and then they told us that before the Germans showed up, all the men and youngsters from 14 and older should sit on the ground with their hands on their heads and not to move.

If we had to move we needed permission, and if we didn't get it we would be sorry. We sat like that, on the ground, probably for two hours. The women were perhaps 150 ft. away and they were told to either sit on the ground or kneel on the ground.

They told us that if we didn't obey, because it was wartime, we would be considered the enemy. We saw the Russian guards changing their uniforms into civilian clothes. They had no idea what fate had in store for them. When I saw the German tanks compared to the smaller Polish tanks I thought to myself, "How can an army like that be defeated?" Finally, the translator told us, "These are orders from the German military. You cannot stay at the border any longer.

You must return to the place you came from to qualify for food rationing cards. Without such cards you will not get food and you will all starve."

Then they let the women come over to our side to be reunited with the families and we picked ourselves up and started to walk. We couldn't walk on the farmers' road because the German military was using it, so we walked in the ditch next to it. We hoped that somehow we might get out of this situation and find a place where we could rest a bit.

We felt that we should separate our family from this huge number of people so that we would not be competing for food and water. That gave us away. The Germans knew we were Jews, because the Jews would run away. The Polish gentiles didn't.

They were spitting at us, calling us many names we didn't understand. We put our heads down and stayed out of trouble and kept on moving. Finally, we were able to find a farm road that was not being used by the Germans. Our parents were at a loss as to what to tell us. We tried not to ask too many questions and not be crybabies. We knew they were under enormous stress because they were trying to protect us.

We looked up to them and all the while we were thinking, "What is our future? Is there a future for us at all? The German army was so powerful!"

CHAPTER 3

The nightmare begins:
Living with the madness

The trip back to Smorgonie was frightening, but being home again gave us a fleeting sense of calm in our familiar surroundings. We found that our house, in addition to many others (about 80% Jewish homes), were all destroyed from either bombings or were purposely torched by neighbors so they could take what they could and blame it on the Germans.

Such was war, they figured. They could find excuses later. We stayed with friends for two weeks and were then told to get ready to report to a ghetto. Every small village with a small Jewish population was moved to another larger village with a larger Jewish population. Then they formed a ghetto within that village.

This was the summer of 1941 and we were with friends of ours whose house was saved. We stayed with them only temporarily. Then the announcement came by radio and by placards that were posted on the town hall that we were to be registered immediately.

We went to the town square (at this time we had no restrictions) where we found out that all the Jews would be required in a week to enter the ghetto. We didn't know what *the ghetto* meant. The ghetto was simply designed to segregate us from the others. The Germans picked out a poor area and would encircle it with barbed wire with one major gate that was guarded by the Lithuanian police and the Jewish police that the Germans had assigned for that duty.

We were told that we could only take what we could carry on our backs with us to our new 'home.' So what do you take when you know you will not be able to go out again? You take the essentials, of course. Food and clothing and more clothing if you should have to trade clothes for food. So we ended up, a family of five put into a single room in a house.

If a house had three or four rooms, it had three or four families living there.

We only had straw sacks for beds. Small children were allowed to be together but not with the adults. The ghetto was under the control of the Jewish police and the Polish police with the Germans controlling both of them.

The Germans required the Jews to form an administrative body, the Jewish Council or *Judenrat*. This governing council would 'represent' all the Jews in the ghetto to their Nazi 'protectors.' The council consisted of about a dozen Jews that were picked by the Germans and who would be given orders. "Orders cannot be disobeyed," they said. "Severe punishment would ensue." We soon found out what they meant by that statement.

The 'protectors' first demanded that all valuables be turned over to them: wedding rings, gold watches, etc. Women with fur jackets had to give them up. Everything of value was turned in. Disobeying the order ensured a harsh penalty which was usually a severe beating which some didn't survive. We lived in a slum area house just outside of town before the ghetto was enclosed and encircled by barbed wire.

We were told that a siren would sound in the morning requiring all of us to report on the street in front of the house for a role call count, an '*appell*.' They said that the punishment for not obeying would be severe. They didn't spell it out but we thought it meant a severe beating.

We were lined up by the Jewish police in groups of one hundred, five by 20, the shorter people in the front, the taller people in the back so they could see everybody. There was always a German Lagerführer in charge.

He would give the instructions to the others who passed them down. They would pass from one house to the other and count the people, make notes and then tell us we could go back to the house.

They also explained that the people who were able to work would be taken outside the ghetto to various areas like Polish public buildings where Germans were housed.

The Lithuanians told us which jobs would be assigned to us, primarily to sweep the streets, work on the farms or cut wood to prepare for the winter months.

It was all new to us and all we knew was that we were forbidden to ask questions. We couldn't sleep, either. We talked endlessly as if we could stave off the inevitable with words. What would tomorrow bring? My parents told us not to despair. We would be given food rations (a slice of bread, some potatoes, some vegetables if available). We would be able to cook our own meals outside. We were still slightly optimistic and had a little hope.

The next morning we looked at the time (we still had a watch). It was almost 6:00am and we were getting ready to go outside. It was a summer day, hot, and we were ready to breathe some fresh air. There were so many men, women, babies and children. You could hear the incessant cries of the little children.

You could also hear the mothers try to comfort them. In our house, the former owner, who was a Jewish farmer, had an elderly mother who was very sick. She had asthma and couldn't breathe. She insisted on having the doors and windows open (we knew she wasn't going to last long). We didn't object; we knew far worse things were coming.

Finally it was 6:00am, not daylight yet, and we were just wondering and praying for some security and for the Almighty to give us some hope. After the sirens sounded, we went outside. Our house was close to the gate which meant that we would be counted among the first. A dozen Jewish policemen, two or three Lithuanian guards and the German Lagerführer were there.

We were lined up and they looked at us, counted us, made their notations and we stayed there. When you heard the siren sound again you could go back to your homes.

We waited to hear it. This was a daily thing. We had no job assignments right away. If they needed say a hundred people, they would come to where we lived. The Jewish police also wore the armband with the Star of David so we knew they were chosen for the job. They said they needed people, "Get outside. If you are physically able to work, get outside."

They would make excuses for the ones who were not able-bodied. They escorted the people and assigned one of the hundred as a 'kapo' (a prison functionary). They were responsible for them. If somebody was missing, they would pay the price for it.

It wasn't too bad for the first few days. In the evening they would bring a farmer's wagon with the rationed food to our house of 22 people. They had already figured out how much we should get. We realized that at least we were getting some food in addition to the food that we had brought with us. The first week we thought that things might even improve.

We heard that they were taking people to other communities to work on farms. They would allow the people that worked on the farms to bring the loose vegetables with them. It was cheaper for the Germans.

During the evening of July 14th, my father and one of my cousins left the house under the cover of darkness to trade some of our belongings for food with the local farmers. While doing so, he and 23 others were arrested by the Lithuanian military. They were all then taken to the woods and summarily executed. Not knowing the fate of my father, we were all worried. He didn't come home that next day.

My mother and my brother went out to look for him and that's when they heard from neighbors that some of the Jews that were rounded up were taken to the woods and murdered. I have never returned to Poland so I don't know if there is a mass grave or any headstone to commemorate their deaths.

All I knew then was that I was without a father. The ache in my heart was unbearable and the loss so strong that my mother was inconsolable. This was the end of my summer and the beginning of my journey to manhood. The ghetto in Smorgon was closed in early 1942 and my family was sent to what was to be the first of many work/concentration camps.

The camps

For the first time in my short life I was leaving my own country. My entire family was uprooted from their hometown in March of 1942. The reason was that my mother was informed that they needed 2,000 people (almost half of the entire ghetto) for a work project. When they realized that they couldn't get 2,000 people they said 1,000 people would be needed to report to a labor camp. My mother and my sister were picked to go.

However, my mother wanted my brother and me to join them because she knew that once we were separated we might not get back together.

We volunteered and they accepted us which meant that two other people could stay. They loaded us all on a cattle wagon because there was a rail line and railway station behind the village. They told us to take along everything we had because they did not know when we would return to the ghetto or be sent somewhere else to another labor camp. We ended up in this place called Orany, not too far from Vilnius. I think we were close to 1,000 people. They separated the men from the women right away.

We arrived at a place where there was a former Jewish synagogue. Next to the synagogue there were three or four private homes that were vacant. My brother and I were housed there. We knew my mother and sister were somewhere but not sure exactly where. My brother and I stayed together, and the next day at the *appell* we could see who remained. We were lucky to see my mother and Rachel and that gave us hope that we would, in the future, be together. This was a labor camp run by the Organisation Todt (OT) which was a private German civil engineering and construction company owned by a man named Fritz Todt.

We were assigned to build a second rail line for the German Wehrmacht (defense force). My brother and I were assigned to the same group but didn't always work together. If they needed men somewhere else they would simply take them. We were always reunited at the end of the day.

At least we knew we were all alive. Size-wise my brother was not large and he was a quiet boy. He tried to be hopeful and be brave and tried to assure me that everything would be okay. We prayed separately for that. He was more hopeful than I was, maybe because he tried harder and pretended more convincingly. He was strong for my sake.

The jobs themselves were always different. At one point, when the work to start building the rail started, they even let us be together to do the job. There were huge nails to be driven and this was hard work but not as hard as distributing the pieces. Three people were assigned to one rail. When we finished our work we were moved around. They spoke German and we soon learned the good and the bad German.

We also had among us those that knew Polish well. Among them were Polish guards. They would be interpreters. No questions could be asked, however. If you did ask a question you would be clobbered.

We managed to do the work and then we were again waiting for the end of the day to place our tools in their boxes and wait for the *appell* again. We were put into the cattle wagons and taken back. Strangely enough, we were not as hungry as we had expected to be perhaps because we were new to the job.

We stretched out on the straw sacks in our barracks and let our bodies begin the next cycle of rest to prepare for the next day's work. There was no rabbi among us, though sometimes a religious person was available. The rabbis were afraid to identify themselves. The Lithuanians and the Germans hated the Jews, our appearance, everything about us. Some of the rabbis even shaved their beards off to hide their identity. There was no Sabbath for any of us. We were available to work at any time.

I think we stayed at Orany for three months. The construction work was finished and we remained throughout the summer and into the fall. We had no calendars. One day was no different than the next or the next after that. Our concern was staying alive. Knowing it was a Wednesday or a Thursday would have made no difference. It was a question of survival.

Thankfully, there were no barking, growling guard dogs. We were not permitted visitors, so we didn't see my mother or sister. They moved us to another camp in November of 1942 where we continued the same type of work. They didn't tell us where we were going but we expected the conditions would be the same. This was in eastern Lithuania.

The name of the place was Ignalina (a place I later heard got its name from two Lithuanian lovers with popular names: Ignas and Lina). The second camp was Swienciany Labor Camp. My brother and I were assigned to do distribution work for a construction company that was building a second rail line so that the Germans had a two-way transport capability to the eastern front and back. We were a group of about 20.

My escape from the airport

The two largest labor groups of men were employed at the railroad station and at the airport. I worked for several weeks at the airport, assigned to a construction company responsible for enlarging the existing facilities. That year, the Germans began to liquidate the smaller ghettos from the surrounding communities. People suitable for work were sent to various labor camps; the elderly, young and sick were exterminated in Ponary, a camp on the outskirts of Vilno or Vilnius.

The Germans told the unfortunate victims that they would be resettled to join their relatives in the ghetto of Vilno or other ghettos. Instead, they were taken to Ponary by the trainload, beaten, shot and unceremoniously dumped at already-prepared mass graves. Several youngsters that were left behind to bury the victims were able to escape. They entered the ghetto, and that's how we were told of the shocking experience.

The Jews in the ghetto realized full-well how vulnerable they were. A few that had the means and opportunity to buy guns, left the ghettos to join the partisans in the nearest woods or formed their own fighting groups. Without arms, no partisan group would let you join them. As we learned after the war, quite a few Jews were robbed by the various partisan groups and lost their lives.

Many were caught by the Germans and shot. In spite of the strict security in the ghetto, there were some secret passages known only to a few. On occasion, the ghetto would be sealed off. No one was permitted in or out, and that usually spelled trouble. House searches, roundups and selections would follow. The Germans suspected that Jewish partisans from the neighboring woods would occasionally enter the ghetto for supplies, ammunition or recruits. When informed, the Germans would spare no effort to apprehend or kill them.

On a certain Friday, while leaving the ghetto for work at the airport, we noticed unusual activities at the gate. Truckloads of German soldiers lined the street outside the ghetto. We suspected something sinister was in the making.

As we kept walking, the soldiers appeared on both sides of our column with rifles on shoulders forming an escort. We knew the escort was not for our protection; we expected and feared the worst.

The word spread rapidly through the grapevine to run and try to escape if it looked like we were headed for annihilation. We were all bound together at that point by our shared fear, something I would experience for the rest of my war years in captivity.

We managed to reach the perimeter of the airport and once inside the gate, we noticed German soldiers camouflaged in the bushes along the fence. The crowd became restless. We heard people shouting, "We are trapped. Let's run now! They will take us to Ponary!" All of a sudden, all hell broke loose.

People from the front columns came running toward us screaming, "They will kill us! Run for your life!" Bullets came at us from all sides. I ran with the others toward the fence. Many people were cut down by the fire from the machine guns mounted on the roofs of the buildings.

We tried to reach the parked cattle cars near the fence to get under cover. Once there, I scaled a six-foot wire fence. I didn't dare look back. Reaching the top, my hands bleeding from the cuts from the wire, I jumped to the ground. While attempting to get up, I turned around. As far as the eye could see, people covered the fence like ants, some caught on the wire and hanging, others jumping or lying on the ground.

The constant firing of the machine guns and the scene around the fence with many fallen bodies resembled a battlefield.

I picked myself up and ran toward the cover of the bushes several hundred feet away. Once there, I felt exhausted and tried to catch my breath, but I knew that I had no time to rest. When I stuck my head up, I saw three escapees coming toward me shouting, "RUN, the Germans are chasing us on motorcycles!"

Getting on my knees, I looked back toward the clearing. Hundreds of people were running, some falling. Then I noticed from the direction of the gate, two motorcycles were heading right toward us. They stopped, put their machine guns on the ground, quickly set them up and started shooting in our direction. We immediately dispersed.

After running for about ten minutes in the woods, I noticed farm houses through the clearing and headed in that direction, thinking it might be a good hiding place or at least a place to rest for a few precious moments.

I reached the nearest barn, and inside there was a large pile of hay in a kind of mezzanine with a bed of straw on the back half. I crawled under the layer of straw, taking care to lie absolutely flat and motionless.

My mind was racing. I tried to assess the situation. I knew the farmer and the Germans would be searching for us. The shrill sound of machine gun fire never left my head for a moment.

Suddenly there were loud voices coming closer to the barn. It was the Germans. They were repeatedly shouting, "Jud e, Jud e!" A group - I don't know how many because my face was flattened in the straw - entered the barn and began to search the pile of hay. After convincing themselves that there were no Jews there, they left in a hurry.

I swear, my heart must have actually stopped beating while they were searching. The farmer and the children stayed to put the pile of hay back together. Then they left, locking the door.

My body was numb. I was able to move a little and stuck my head out of the dusty straw for air. I was in shock and couldn't think straight. After a while, I looked around and noticed I was not alone in the barn. Chickens were moving around freely. At that point I would have loved to have traded places with any one of them. I realized the cows that were in the pasture would soon be returning to the barn at sunset and I decided to move over to the hay stack for the night.

While I was buried in the hay stack, many questions racked my brain. Where do I go from here? Is the ghetto still in existence or liquidated? If there is no ghetto, and my family is gone, what is the point of trying to stay alive? What happened to the people trapped at the airport?

Are they somewhere on their way to a labor camp or taken to Ponary? In the evening, the farmer brought the cows in and locked the doors. I decided to leave the barn before sunrise. Though I was exhausted and hungry, I could not sleep, and the night dragged on like eternity. I climbed on top of the mezzanine, was able to break loose a few of the boards, just enough to squeeze through, and jumped to the ground.

I had no sense of direction. All I wanted to find out was what had happened to the ghetto, but I was afraid to be recognized and turned over to the Germans. To stay out of sight, I ran toward the woods. After a while, I reached a clearing and saw an elderly man watching a herd of cows.

I decided to take a chance and walked over to him. I needed no introduction; he recognized the Star of David immediately. He looked me over and questioned me about where I was coming from. I pointed to the direction of the farms and asked him what he knew about the ghetto. He told me the ghetto was still there and that the people from the airport were all taken to Estonia.

He broke off a piece of bread from his loaf, gave it to me, saying, "Keep by the railroad track, it will lead you to the city." I followed his advice and reached the outskirts of the city. On one street, I came to a bridge that was guarded by a soldier. I turned in the opposite direction and then heard a horse and wagon coming toward me. A farmer was delivering produce to the market. He stopped the horse when he saw me and said, "Are you from the airport? A lot of people were killed there, the rest were taken to Estonia."

I told him I was trying to make my way to the ghetto, but a soldier was guarding the bridge. I offered him my watch if he would let me get on the wagon. He thought for a few seconds and then told me to rip the Star of David from my jacket and he said, "Crawl under the canvas." He greeted the soldier while passing the bridge, and after ten minutes of silence, I heard him asking me if I wanted to get off now or wait until we reached a major street.

I was grateful to this man for his help. Before I left the wagon, he said to me, "I knew a lot of Jewish people. Too bad what is happening to them. You are not far from the ghetto gate." It must have been around 7:00am. I waited by one of the gates and heard the sound of people marching. As the column got closer, I recognized them. They were Jews returning from a night's work to the ghetto. I joined them.

One man gave me his overcoat to put on my shoulders because I had removed the Star of David from my jacket earlier. To enter the ghetto, the Star of David had to be visible. Thankfully, I made it inside and I was reunited with my mother, brother and sister for a few more months.

Size matters

One of my jobs was to distribute the parts that would go to build this rail line. That included rail ties and also the metal that went under it. A wet rail tie is very heavy.

Even though they assigned three people to carry it on their shoulders, they would frequently drop it, and then they would have to return and take another one. I was among those three people.

There is probably an ancient story that addresses this subject more eloquently, but I will just tell it in my own words. I was not tall when I was a teenager. Matter of fact I was short. Being short, I couldn't be in the front or the back of the railroad tie; I had to be in the middle. The taller people, on the front and back, would always carry more weight and when the tie was hoisted up on their shoulders I couldn't even reach it from my vantage point in the middle!

Consequently, my workload was light but my food rations of bread and soup were the same as everybody else's. The other fellows really needed twice as many calories as me to fuel their work but they didn't get it. They were deprived, getting only 800 or 900 calories/day. Their health suffered more. It was inevitable.

In Ignalina, we lived in real barracks, and it was the first time we were able to talk with my mother and sister. They had faced similar conditions to those my brother and I experienced. In addition to working on the railroad, some of the women were assigned to work in the military kitchen. This was considered like a bonus. They were very pleased to have a job with access to more food AND they could also stay together.

There was a group of four people: my mother, sister, my aunt and niece. This camp was more difficult. It was a bigger camp with Poles, White Russians. We Jews were also kept separate. If someone during the occupation committed a crime, they would put them in a labor camp. A period of time there seemed shorter because the work was very advanced and we finished it, quickly. The winter of 1942 we were returned to the ghetto of Vilna for a few months.

This was a new ghetto for me and it didn't seem particularly bad compared to Smorgon. In the summer of 1943, we were moved by rail to the Goldfield and Vaivara Labor Camps near Ereda in Estonia where we dug test wells for the extraction of shale deposits.

On the way we heard rumors that the Germans were primarily interested in destroying us and not using us for labor anymore. This wasn't a subject that anyone wanted to talk about as we were worried that we would end up in Ponary (near Vilnius) a place where 70,000 Jews were murdered by the Nazis from 1941-44. They ended up taking us to the Vaivara Concentration Camp (the largest of the 22 concentration camps in Estonia) because in Estonia they had large deposits of shale in the ground.

The Germans had discovered a way of extracting oil from shale deposits, and since they had free labor to do it, why not use it (us)? We were assigned to dig the test wells.

We began by digging four or five feet down and immediately the hole started filling up with water. Because the test well was huge, we would go down to maybe 12 feet until the shale deposits were reached.

Most of the workers were young men. We arrived early in the morning carrying our picks and shovels with us and we would start a fire because it was winter. They had huge pumps that were connected to the outside electricity. They were pumping water out of the holes. However, there was still knee-high water left and we were soaked to the bone working in the cold.

Every 15-20 minutes (there were three people working in this area), they would hoist us up and we would take off our shoes and wring out the rags we wore to warm up a bit. The water was pumped out, and as long as we could see the shale, it was not level.

We would break up the shale with an iron bar and put it in the pail and it would be hoisted up while another pail was lowered. The Lithuanian guards were always unhappy and yelled at us in German to speed up to meet our quota. (The guards would suffer if we didn't meet our quota.)

At the end of the day, at around 4:00pm, the work would stop and we'd dry our feet before we began the 3-5 mile walk back to the camp in the cold. The barracks were flimsy and you could feel the cold penetrating the thin barrack walls.

We had lights out at 8:00pm. After a few weeks, we started losing weight...and our strength. It had now gone beyond simply enduring the work; it was a matter of sheer survival. We lived from hour to hour because we didn't know what to expect.

We looked for signs that would tell us what was going on. One of those was when instead of our normal ration of a single slice of bread we got a loaf. That meant we would be packing up and traveling.

That's when prayers came in handy. Separated from my mother and sister now in Estonia I didn't know what had become of them. Life could end for them or for me at any time. It was a terrible anxiety. We had no calendars that could tell us when we would be set free, if ever. We had regressed to the primitive animal stage. We were now only concerned with food. It alone governed our every thought. Our stomachs had finally taken over. We were in deep survival mode.

After the work in Estonia was finished, the Germans put us on a merchant boat in Tallinn, and we traveled for about three days. It was sea-sickening. As soon as we got on the boat we couldn't keep any food down. The ship pitched and bounced constantly. It was terrible. Finally, we made it to a port. I think it was Danzig. They rushed us out of there and we walked for about three or four hours, guarded by the Lithuanians.

We thought this might be our last walk. We couldn't ask any questions and they wouldn't volunteer any information. It seemed like we had walked forever. Finally, in October 1943, we reached Stutthof (some 20 miles east of Danzig) and we saw enormous lights.

The closer we got to the gate I saw a sign over the gate that read, "Arbeit macht das Leben suess" (Work makes life sweet).

We were rushed along by the guards because they were tired, too. We entered the camp and we noticed on the fence there were sentry posts with machine guns. Every 40-50 ft. there were guards in towers. We saw a canal about 8 feet wide outside the fence. It wasn't for drainage; it was to prevent escape. The armed guards walked the perimeter with their dogs.

It left me with the impression that as bad as things were, worse things were yet to come. I was separated from my brother at that point. We were like a herd of cattle, like zombies. Not really alive but not quite dead, either. The ones that fell back and couldn't keep up were beaten. Many people fell on the ground, lifeless, after their beatings.

We didn't know what happened to them, but dead or alive, the numbers needed to match, and I'm sure our officious Nazi captors made the numbers add up. To the right side of the camp was a huge building with a mammoth chimney. This was directly above the ovens where they took the dead to be incinerated.

I remember a terrible stench coming from the smokestack. It was the unmistakable rancid smell of the newly dead. It literally tied my stomach up in knots. There were barracks ready for us that held a hundred people or more. The camp was enormous with many barracks, but many were empty, due to the recent victims. My only worry was my brother's whereabouts. Did he make it or not?

That single fear plagued me all night. I prayed that someone had seen him or knew him and could tell me if he made it alright.

Stutthof was so immense that there was no way a family could have stayed together. So I told myself he was alive and fell asleep until the next morning when the same procedure played itself out again. Siren. Line-up. Be counted.

The weather was cold, but I was lucky to have a fairly good pair of shoes. Upon processing in to a camp, a person went into the shower, gave the guards his old clothes (which you didn't get back), was issued a pair of shoes and striped clothing without underwear.

I had no proper coat but a kind of cast-off military garment. It kept me fairly warm. A couple days later, I heard there was a Jewish group that was kept separate, away from us, all wearing the Star of David of course. Some prisoners wore triangles. A red triangle meant that you were a political prisoner. The other triangles had their meanings, too, but we never found out what they were.

This separate Jewish group changed in size. Some people became ill, and if the Germans needed people they would take them from other groups. When they chose us the *kapos* said, "Take off the Star of David. We need you but keep it in your pocket until you get back to your barrack."

We could only keep it off when we worked. The work could be anything, like cleaning the fence area or even work on the local farms. This was a bonus because it meant that you could find a carrot or something and take it with you. There were no light moments. Life at Stutthof was like a perpetual eclipse of the sun. Darkness shrouded our every thought. Resignation to death in captivity was our ideology. We were limited to gatherings of ten people in a group, even outside. We were not permitted to worship or to celebrate any of our holy days.

Life in Stutthof was miserable to say the least. When I found my brother, I rejoiced at being able to get together with him. I told the *kapo* in my barrack that I found my brother and that we would like to be together. "Could we?" His answer was, "What can I get for it?" Some people had some things in hiding, silver spoons or rings that could be payment for such *favors*. I promised him that if I got an extra quart of soup I would give it to him.

He was a sympathetic fellow and said, "Bring your brother over and make sure you two stay together." Sometimes the people in charge would overlook this type of reunion. We were happy.

Filip and I now had a double bunk and some hope to go with it. One day, it might have been a holiday, we didn't go to work, so we were allowed to sit outside the barrack and relax. We were all talking together. We dared to bring up the subject, "What do you think you will do if you survive?"

The average person's dream was to be a farmer, baker, grocer, anything connected with food. There were constant flows of people coming in to the camp. It was an extermination camp.

From Stutthof they took us to the cities of Aurich and Meppen (both around 30,000 people in Lower Saxony) to dig anti-tank trenches because the Germans were expecting the second front - the Americans and the British - to attack them. Again, my diminutive size helped me survive. People that were physically stronger or taller were at a disadvantage.

The *kapos* positioned themselves by the holes where we were digging anti-tank trenches. There were hundreds of thousands of people as far as the eye could see. It was just a massive group of people doing the digging. Although the Germans had tractors and other equipment, an army needs fuel for such work, and they figured they could use us, instead.

After all, why waste perfectly good fuel when you have slave workers?

Imagine people digging 10-15 foot trenches by hand! We had several layers of people digging from the bottom. Then they moved the earth to a higher level which was three feet higher until it was finally moved to the upper level and dispersed. People would push wheelbarrows alongside and then stop there to fill them up, day after day. Other people would fill their wheelbarrow and then move on to the next one. It was a human chain situation. You couldn't rest. There was a *kapo* with a big stick who kept repeating, "Keep on moving. Keep on moving."

We would occasionally see someone, a man that was tall man and in good shape. Why was he in such good shape? It was because they had just brought him in from another ghetto and he hadn't as yet experienced this hard work.

These were the people that succumbed to sickness first. It was too much of a shock for their system. The strong will become weak. It's like a big Belgian draught horse next to a smaller horse that is half its size, skinny, almost ready to drop dead. Who will the farmer use first? The big one!

So people's liabilities outside the camps (like my small size) were an asset inside. The Germans were, if anything, predictable. "Ordnung muss sein" (order is a must) meant that procedures were uniform in every concentration camp. And you could set your watch by them (if you still had a watch or if you even cared).

The end pieces

A day at Stutthof started with the *appell*. Then the count was matched against the barrack roster. Then we would line up for breakfast. Most of the time it was a single slice of bread sometimes with margarine.

Just imagine a loaf of bread that was divided into 12 slices. The end pieces were bigger than the middle ones so everybody wanted one of them. That meant that everybody became an Einstein trying to figure out how to get the coveted crust! Just imagine a line of maybe a hundred people - one barrack at a time - that is lined up to get a slice of bread.

You come to the window and there was a guy inside - also a prisoner of war - that would simply push out the slice of bread for you. You took it and you had to move on.

But how do you get an end piece? It was actually pretty simple in theory. If I saw that a new loaf was brought out and was about to be cut, I would count the number of people in line. If I was about a dozen places away from the window then the chances were pretty good of me grabbing an end piece.

If I could see that there was no chance for me to get it, I would get out of the line and go to the end of it (this was very much against the rules and if the *kapo* saw you doing this he would beat you for it).

It all came down to calories. An end piece was about a slice and a half and that was incentive enough for people to snag one. It actually got rather comical watching people hop out of line and then back in, just before they got to the window. It's amazing what we will do to stay alive. I'm reminded of that every time I look at a loaf of freshly baked bread.

In September of 1944, my brother and I were taken by train from Stutthof to Neuengamme (a concentration camp near Hamburg that was built in 1935). From there we walked to the job site. We worked at this job, digging anti-tank trenches, for four months until the work in the area was completed.

Neuengamme was a better camp than Stutthof because it was strictly a work camp and not an extermination camp. There they treated us as laborers.

Then one day we were given a loaf of bread, an unmistakable signal that we were moving on. Sure enough, they were taking us back to Stutthof.

At this point, we were so exhausted and sick that we couldn't really work anymore and didn't really care where they sent us. The war was coming to an end. This was the fall of 1944. My brother and I were together. The fact that I was still alive against all odds gave me hope that I could stay alive.

Some of the prisoners who were working on the nearby farms had picked up a discarded magazine or newspaper (though they had no right to do so). After reading the headlines, they could see what was going on.

The headlines told of German cities being bombed and Germany losing the war. The German army was being depleted of its soldiers, its materiel and its resolve, and that made us feel a bit better. I felt that the odds were maybe in my favor and that, God willing, I might survive and be able to live for maybe a few more years.

There were all sorts of people in Stutthof: political prisoners, Jehovah's Witnesses, gypsies, homosexuals and others. In short, everybody that the Germans didn't like was there.

Once, some people had gone missing and a punishment had to be meted out. They took everybody outside and told us to stay there for hours and hours. The weather was so brutal that I don't know how I stood it. We clung to each other to stay warm. The people from the outside line exchanged places with those on the inside. Nothing seemed to help.

Many things went through my mind like a beating I had once received in Smorgonie. The Germans took us to unload some food from a train and we were carrying it from the wagon and stacking it in piles.

I heard from others that there was one barrack that had some containers with marmalade and other things. People were helping themselves, so I did the same. I ate as much as I could.

Then we saw one angry German guard cross the platform and he caught us. He screamed and cursed and took out his rifle and started to chase us. Finally he took the three of us.

He ordered us to stand facing the barrack and to count in German. I remember I heard the others counting and when we reached the number nine we heard a shot. I thought I had taken a bullet. I was in a state of shock. I didn't know what to think. I heard more shots. They were trying to scare us.

The guard said, "Turn around, you. I will give you a break this time, but if this happens again you will face the consequences." He came over to me and slapped my face several times and slammed the butt of the rifle on my rear and said, "Go back to work." I knew I deserved it because I had disobeyed the orders. The other two boys got beaten too.

CHAPTER 4

Finding strength:
Why do they hate us so?

From the moment my family and I were forced from our home and fled to the Russian border carrying what little we could on our backs and on my brother's bicycle, I asked myself two questions. The first was, "Do I have the strength to endure what will come?

The second was, "Why do the Germans, the Russians and even some of my own countrymen hate us so?" The first question was answered in April of 1945 when I was liberated from my captors and saw the light of freedom reflected in the eyes of the British army soldiers who freed me. The second question has perplexed me until this very day, some 75 years later.

The challenge of finding strength was a daily occurrence in my waking <u>and</u> sleeping hours. During the day, I practiced the art of making myself invisible to my guards, shriveling my physical self to nothing so as not to be noticed. This was made easier by the meager rations of food we received and by the sheer mass of humanity that surrounded me.

Thousands of my fellow Jewish prisoners could never be fully invisible as they, too, were forced to wear the bright yellow Star of David on their clothes and because we were all segregated into special barracks that only housed those of my faith. We were the lowest of the low, lower than political prisoners, lower than the gypsies, lower than the homosexuals or *deviants* as the Germans called them.

Forbidden to practice our faith or even pray openly, all the prayers and thoughts we had of better times and freedom were forced inward, deep into the recesses of our minds never to escape our mouths. We became the stateless, the ostracized, pariahs that the Third Reich had so labeled us.

We were responsible, in our captors' eyes, for all the ills that had befallen the Fatherland which was why Jewish shops and homes across Germany, my native Poland and so many other European countries were looted of their possessions.

My people's wealth, livelihood and most of all their future were destroyed in a matter of a few years.

We were left with only a stigma that the yellow Star of David now symbolized on our jackets. Our names were no longer important, only the numbers burned into our arms like cattle brands served to distinguish us from each other except when we stood to be counted in the early morning hours before leaving for our forced labor.

I kept telling myself, "My name is Aron, my name is Aron. I am a young man. I am son of my parents. I am a Polish citizen from Smorgonie. I am a human being and a Jew." This litany was like a mantra I chanted in my head, safe from the prying eyes and ears of the Nazis. It was my own personal affirmation of my existence. It was something no one could take from me no matter how insignificant and anonymous they would try to make me.

The search for strength was only superseded by my fixation on food, something all of us in the camps shared. The desire for just one more piece of bread, a thin slice of potato or a few more sips of liquid was like a swirling cloud in my head. It became almost unbearable, especially as my physical strength started to slowly slip away.

The need to survive one more day until the next meal was ever-present. The desire for food even crept into my dreams and took over my sleep. In one recurring dream, I sat at a lavish table all decked out with my mother's cooking and was surrounded by my family.

When my plate was empty, my mother would come and fill it up, saying, "Aron, you must eat some more. You are a growing boy and you need your nourishment!" I willingly obliged her by taking another helping and then, feeling full, pushed myself away from the table along with my brother and sister to escape the house for a few hours of play.

That dream was usually shattered by the noise of the *kapos* as they rousted us out of our beds once again to stand for the *appell*.

A person learns how to conserve his strength, especially when the threat of death by overexertion or starvation presents itself. You work slower, swing your pick with less deliberation, walk with smaller, more measured steps and speak softer whenever you speak. Every stitch of clothing and especially shoes that chafe can be an assailant, robbing you of your comfort and maybe even your health.

Create a blister and it can inhibit your movements and cause the guards to beat you for moving too slowly. When the blisters pop they can get infected, and with little or no medical attention at the ready, infections can turn ugly and create bigger problems.

In a strange way, being constantly aware of these things, made the time pass more quickly and that made the workday seem a bit shorter than it really was. The mind is a wonderful escape route from reality. I am sure that all of us concocted our own parallel universe in our heads.

I am also sure that my fellow prisoners, played the piano, went on ocean cruises and caressed their loved ones in their minds, every single day. I know that my mind carried many of the same kinds of thoughts as my physical body carried buckets of sludge and shale from the hundreds of holes we dug.

While my mind was removing me from my situation it was also reminding me that the world of my carefree youth lay outside the wooden barrack walls and still farther outside the barbed wire fence. No amount of wishing could help me to the other side. Some could not cope with such long-term confinement and tried to escape. They were promptly caught, beaten, hung or shot, often in front of our eyes.

All of us secretly muttered under our breath from time to time that, 'they were the lucky ones.'

Being so young, I didn't feel that kind of deep depression because the world I left behind, the world of a teenager, bore no mark of my presence. I hadn't really done anything to miss nor had I any love to regret except for the loss of my family. My life was still pretty much a blank canvas, and it looked with each passing day that my imprisonment would prevent me from showing the world that I had even existed.

Being imprisoned in war time is probably pretty much like being in prison in peacetime except that all of us were not serving a specific sentence with a date certain for our release. Our crime was simply being Jewish and there was no pardon for that crime.

Indeed, our status pretty much allowed our captors to accuse us of anything they wanted and to use any trumped up charge to end our lives at will with no judge or jury to review our pleas.

Our situation was also like that of soldiers on a battlefield. While we depended on each other, knowing each other too well was often painful, but it was the only human thing to do. When a prisoner died from natural causes or from a beating or hanging it was like losing a family member, because one of us had gotten to know him well and that meant his death affected us all. To me, this was really a great paradox.

Our individual will to survive existed alongside the pursuit of a collective responsibility for one another. Like two parallel swiftly running streams it is perhaps the best symbol of the duality of our existence on this earth. The Jewish people (and the Jewish religion) have survived by passing down history to one another, so it was not at all unusual for prisoners to confide the most intimate details of their lives with one another.

By doing that, the stories became more real and had a chance of living on in another person's memory. And, if that person were to perish in captivity, we would carry his story with us so that it wouldn't die with him. That gave us some hope and some strength and made us realize that we were never really alone.

If I am to be honest, I cannot credit finding or maintaining my strength to the tactics I employed or even to the people around me. I must credit God and Him alone for giving me the will to survive.

The answer to the second question about hate is one that has been on every Jewish person's mind since Jews first suffered persecution. I suppose that like any human emotion, hatred cannot be fully explained and certainly never justified. But to deny its existence and not confront it or its root causes is to stick one's head in the sand and pretend, that like a summer storm, it would soon blow over.

The Holocaust of the Second World War made it impossible for anyone, anymore, to ignore the level of hatred the Nazis had for us. Indeed, the hatred was widespread and knew no physical borders. It included those who were 'different,' wherever they lived. This 'special' kind of hatred for the Jews had been fomenting for a long, long time in Europe and had not only traveled through countries but was passed on from generation to generation, from father to son.

It manifested itself in the Nuremberg Laws and gave the Nazis carte blanche to pursue their quest for our extermination – the 'final solution' as they called it.

For me, personally, I have no room for hatred in my heart. I cannot bring myself to despise whole groups of people. I cannot envy their good fortune or be jealous of their wealth. I don't ascribe evil motives to entire nations or religious or ethnic groups.

I was not brought up to hate and I will never lift one finger in its defense.

Yes, I know there is evil in the world, just as I know there is goodness. Man has a free will to choose to live in the light of that goodness or hide his evil intentions in the darkness of hypocrisy. My faith has sustained me through my years of incarceration and subjugation by men who believed in their inherent right to rule over others...and to take the lives of innocent people as they saw fit.

While I still do not fully understand this kind of blind pointless hatred, I must accept that it exists and that it must never be allowed to gain even an inch of ground in the fight for goodness, fairness and the rights of all men to live free of persecution.

CHAPTER 5

Three Liberations:
Release and reunification

Liberation 1: My mother and sister

I didn't know that my mother and sister were free until I wrote to my aunt in Israel (the only address I could remember) telling her of my own liberation. My aunt's husband worked at the Rotenberg Electric Plant in Haifa and I knew his name. I figured I would write to this address and tell him who I was and that maybe there was a chance we could be connected through him.

Amazingly, the letter got there and set off a chain of events. (I would see them after my liberation). My uncle would later tell me that while he was working he heard his name come over the company loudspeaker. He was told to drop what he was doing and come to the office. His supervisor said that they had a letter for him from Europe. Like many people, he assumed that this was a letter telling them that no one survived.

They gave him the letter, and I'm sure that his hands trembled as he opened it. Upon seeing that it was written in Yiddish he was extremely anxious to read it, but my uncle couldn't read Yiddish. He could only read Hebrew.

He ran home and showed it to my aunt who read the letter that said, "I, Aron, am alive. I am in Bergen-Belsen and all I know is that I'm alive. What happened to my mother and sister I do not know." Actually, my mother and Rachel ended up in the Jewish community of Lodz in Poland.

Little did I know that my mother had done the same thing; she wrote to her sister, my aunt, and said that she and my sister were alive but said that they didn't know what happened to Aron and Filip! So my aunt wrote to me and said that they would like to join me in Bergen-Belsen. My mother, sister and nieces were liberated together by the Russian forces after the fall of Berlin.

Thankfully, my mother spoke Russian very well and the Russian forces were actually advancing to Berlin so she could communicate with them. Among the soldiers were a few Russian officers. When one of these officers, a colonel who happened to be Jewish, found these former prisoners and was informed that there were some Jewish women that might be among them, he said that they were free and could go home.

He, himself, had to move on, but he put this little camp of a hundred in the charge of another Russian officer who stayed in the camp with them. Needless to say, my mother and sister were glad to be alive and have food and clothing. This was not far from Berlin. They were still required to work and were taken to work by the Russian officer and made to clean up the cities that had been bombed.

After work they would be taken back to the camp. Unfortunately, the Russians considered them to be counter-revolutionaries. They said, "Instead of fighting the Germans you were working for them; you helped them!" About a week later, a truck pulled up in the city where they worked and two soldiers in Polish uniforms got out and surveyed the area. They observed the people and listened to what they were saying.

Then they called over a lady and said, "There are many Jewish women among you, correct?," to which the lady said, "Yes, that is true. There are at least four I know," and she pointed out my mother and her family.

The soldiers said, "We are Jewish soldiers in the Polish Army and you must get away from here. If you don't, you may end up in a Russian prison camp or even worse. You are considered counter-revolutionaries by the Russians. My mother asked what she should do. The soldiers said that they she and the others should arrange to come back next week, to the same place, and they would meet them there.

They were advised not to go back to their barrack and that they (the soldiers) would take them to the Jewish community of Lodz which they did.

My mother, my sister, aunt and niece were the beneficiaries of some extraordinary kindness by these Polish army personnel who helped them escape by truck from their camp. I am convinced (and so was my mother AND the soldiers) that they would have eventually been sent to Siberia. They didn't pay these soldiers for their help, but my mother did use some cigarettes that she had hidden away to hire a guide to take them across the Czech border into Munich.

It was a dangerous plan because the guide himself at one point wanted to *have* my sister and my mother, but my mother said, "Nothing doing." They gave him more cigarettes so that he could buy vodka instead. When he fell asleep they took off.

They desperately wanted to join me in Bergen-Belsen. But Feldafing was on the way there and it was a big camp where survivors had gathered. It was a clearing house for information, but just a stopping-off place. Despite that, I set out to meet them and I met a former neighbor of mine from Smorgonie in Bergen-Belsen. She said we couldn't just sit there waiting for them to find us.

We had to go out and find them, so we went to the train and we got on it by bribing the conductors with cigarettes. At the American zone we had to change trains because of the difference in the rail gauge. We boarded the other train and came to Munich, and my neighbor told me she would take me to the Feldafing camp and that she would try to look for them while she looked for her own brother.

It was there, that by some stroke of fate, I met some of my former neighbors from across the street in Smorgonie who had survived.

They were as pleased to see me as I was to see them! I told them about my mother and sister and that I had decided not to wait around for them to find me.

As I said before, little did I know that my mother had already written to her sister in Israel and told her that she and my sister were alive but said that they had no idea what happened to Aron and Filip. It was a tremendous surprise when my aunt wrote to me and said that my mother and sister would like to join me in Bergen-Belsen at the same time we were looking for them in Feldafing!

It was a hot summer day and the place was full of people, and whenever new people came we would greet them and ask them questions. As I was telling them my story, from behind me, a woman clapped her hands and said, "Oh, my God. I saw a daughter and her mother in this camp yesterday and she said that she had a son in Bergen-Belsen and she is trying to get there to meet him!"

I said, "Get me a sandwich or two because I want to go back to the train to Bergen-Belsen to try to find them because there is a danger that if they don't find me there they will go somewhere else."

The train ride back to Bergen-Belsen took two days. We stopped in Celle and from there I waited for a ride to the train station to Bergen-Belsen. I walked from the station straight to the camp. All the while, my anticipation and excitement (and worry) was beginning to make me really nervous.

When I arrived at the camp it was blisteringly hot and I was de-hydrated. In the camp, I shared a room with a young Polish friend of mine who was informed that I was on my way back and would be there at a certain hour. Little did I know that my mother had found my friend and that he had told her that she and my sister should wait at a special place while he went out to find me.

He found me, exhausted from the trip. He ran toward me and he was smiling. I could see this from far away. He was clapping his hands as if he had won the lottery!

He yelled at me, "Aron, Aron, your mother and sister are here!" He told me to wait downstairs. He didn't want them to be too shocked without adequate preparation. He went up and told them I was outside and he took them out to the front of the barrack to meet me. Seeing them both was like being resurrected, for them and for me.

There was a big bench in front, and my friend said to me, "This is a very private moment. I will come back to get you in a little while." The first question my mother asked was, "Did you find out what happened to your brother?" I said, "Yes. I know what happened but the news is not good." I told her that we could go to the hospital in Rotenburg and that we could get the latest information from them. At this point we didn't know he had died. My mother needed to rest for a couple of days before making the trip.

I had stayed in Bergen-Belsen after the liberation along with thousands of others. We stayed there because the housing and medical attention was good and it wouldn't have been sensible for thousands of displaced people to wander aimlessly looking for relatives. Better to have us all in one area.

Bergen-Belsen was an eerie place. They had kept the gas chambers and crematorium so that they could show it to the Germans to prove that atrocities had been committed there, but later they decided to level it. Our barrack was one of hundreds and it was within walking distance to the crematorium. The allies brought many survivors to Bergen-Belsen because of its infrastructure.

The past was moving away as fast as the future was coming for all of the 7,000-8,000 of us there. The British were very kind and tried to help us look for family members.

There were very few translators. The British felt that we would have an easier time of it by using our own camp connections, so they gave us the freedom to do it on our own. I ended up staying at Bergen-Belsen for three whole years before eventually emigrating to the United States.

We had civilian people from Israel that would come to the camp to keep us busy and to give us training, teaching us trades/skills we could use when we left. There were religious organizations that worked with us to help us re-discover our religion. They had meetings and gatherings in the evenings that gave us an opportunity to be together and feel our religious roots again.

Much of their work was directed to helping us re-build our lives and to think about the future, something we had nearly given up hope of realizing after so many years in captivity. I left there in 1949 after the state of Israel was formed. As a matter of fact, I was signed up to go to Israel because my mother had re-married a man from the camp and was leaving for Israel with my sister. They wanted me to come with them.

I declined, feeling that my chances for a new life lay somewhere else. I just didn't know where at that point. Later, as luck would have it, I met a wonderful girl from the camp, Judy, who would later become my wife.

There were two German doctors that worked in the camp and who took care of our medical needs, both physical and emotional. There were, as you might imagine, thousands suffering from trauma and severe emotional problems.

Both doctors were former prisoners of war themselves. I believe they were Jehovah's Witnesses, pacifists. Though we were free, we still needed permission to leave the camp and return. There was a political reason for that...Palestine was still under the British rule.

The Arabs were very much against the Jews coming to Israel because they feared if England would allow a huge segment of these people to go to Palestine they would have more 'enemies.' That led to an agreement limiting the Jewish exodus to Palestine until the State of Israel was established.

We all knew that situation was a temporary one even though it might take years to settle.

I never wanted to go back to Smorgonie because there were still many Jewish haters there. There was a time when my uncle who was in the Russian army (though he was a Polish citizen) was given permission to come back to Poland after the war. He went back to Smorgonie, but after two or three days they told him, "Herschel, if you know what's good for you, you will get out of here because your life is in danger." The Polish people didn't want any witnesses to what they had done with the Jews' property.

There were many stories about former neighbors who had committed acts of destruction against the homes of the Jews which had been occupied by the Nazis.

There was another problem that dogged us. None of us had any official papers, no birth certificates, nothing to prove our identity. The British gave us permission to make new documents with the help of witnesses. If you could find two witnesses that would attest to knowing you and could vouch for where you lived, the British accepted this as a legal document.

When the State of Israel was established, my mother and my sister were incarcerated by the British. This was while they were on their way to Israel with a large group of people. Their ship was stopped and they were taken to Cyprus. While there, my mother was told that her chances of coming to Israel would be better if she were younger.

My mother was born in 1900 and was 49 years old at the time. She was told that if she found two witnesses that would corroborate that she was 40 instead of 49 (because Israel needed young people, not grandmothers), her chances were considerably better at getting an onward passage.

That's exactly what she did! She became a young lady overnight, but she would face the consequences later on when I brought her over to America after I became a citizen.

She used the same documents in America until it was time for her to retire, but she couldn't receive any benefits until I reached out to Senator McCormack from Massachusetts. I explained why she altered her documents, and he was very sympathetic and helpful. This was in 1955 after I had become a citizen myself. For my part, it took me 6-12 months to fully regain my health. I can remember that even though I was gaining weight I always had the feeling of being hungry or worrying about my next meal. Without Judy at my side to help me through this terrible time, I don't know if I could have done it as swiftly.

Liberation 2: Filip and me

My big brother Filip and I were fortunate to have stayed paired up throughout several years of the war. He and I spent months and months of our lives on work details, shuffled from one work camp to another, in our barrack, but with the war winding down something was bound to happen to end our 'prison partnership.'

Since our initial flight from Smorgonie with our parents, Filip and I experienced more together in just a few years than many people share in a lifetime. In the spring of 1945, with the Germans rapidly losing the war, the mood in the camps was changing – among the prisoners and the guards.

In Stutthof, Filip and I heard stories from prisoners who had been able to read some newspaper accounts as they were working off-site of the camp. The news wasn't good for the Germans. They were losing the war and Hitler had gotten desperate and recruited young boys and old men to serve in the place of the fallen German soldiers.

The Russians and the Americans were advancing on Berlin. At the end of March, we were once again to be moved. We were given a loaf of bread and margarine and were readied for travel in cattle wagons. This time it was standing room only. At certain stations, the train would stop to remove the dead prisoners and give us a chance to drink some water. We hadn't a clue as to our destination.

We left Stutthof apparently because the guards didn't know what to do with us. They were being encircled by the opposing armies. They moved us back and forth, back and forth. They hadn't any orders to get rid of us and no orders to keep us.

We were in a perilous situation. People were dying in our wagons of malnutrition and of pure exhaustion. Then we stopped. Unable to move, we were dragged out of the wagons and placed on the ground. Then the empty train took off. It was a cold dark night and we were more dead than alive.

Most of us thought what a relief it would be to face the end of our lives right then and there. We must have laid there for hours. Finally, orders were given. "Move. Move." Those who could walk tried to help the others who couldn't. This unbelievable group of ghosts moved in slow motion, some upright, some on their hands and knees. How long and how far was impossible for us to estimate as we had lost all track of time.

We finally reached a place with some buildings that were under construction. Once inside, we crawled into the unfinished foundation and immediately fell asleep.

The next morning we did get some soup and bread from the guards, but just how long we lay in these 'open graves' I do not know. There were literally thousands of sick prisoners requiring medical attention. One morning we heard an otherworldly noise, a massive rumbling of the ground. It sounded like a combination of an earthquake and a tornado in one. Tanks were on the move.

In the afternoon of April 16th, while we were both stretched out on the ground trying to rest, Filip began to vomit from the effects of dysentery. He was in severe pain. Despite his weakened state, he tried to give me encouragement, and I tried to give it right back to him. We agreed that we both needed to hang on because we had heard that the Lithuanian guards had fled. Freedom was surely coming and coming soon!

Suddenly, the doors of our barrack were pushed open and we heard loud voices and pistol shots. With their guns in their hands, a group of soldiers, maybe a dozen, came into our barrack. We knew they were not German military. From my vantage point, lying on the ground and looking straight up, the soldiers looked like giants from outer space.

One called out for one of his fellow soldiers who spoke Polish to come over. The man had tears in his eyes as he spoke to us. He said, "It is so good to see you alive. We will help you to get well, each and every one of you. This is the British army setting you free. We wish you well. Now we must move on to check every barrack." Though we wanted desperately to shake their hands, we couldn't even lift ourselves from our prone position. Exhaustion was mixed with elation.

Our emotions were a combination of relief, joy and sadness for those who couldn't be there to experience this event so long awaited. Indeed, it was like being in a dream and looking down on yourself as you slept. Was this reality or were our minds playing one last insidious trick on us as life departed our bodies?

No, it was real and Filip and I just looked at each with the same expression on our faces, an expression of gratitude for being spared death.

In the afternoon, the British military ordered several hundred German women to wash our bodies with soap and warm water. They gave us underwear and placed us all on stretchers. It was a moment I will never forget, but I could not fall asleep not knowing what happened to my brother (he had been moved to another barrack because of his acute condition). When I was able to get dressed I left the barrack with one thought, where will I find my brother?

I walked from one tent to another, one barrack to another, looking in people's faces, asking questions and getting discouraged. After a few hours, I felt faint and returned to my barrack. Several of us had contracted dysentery because of the canned food we received. Our stomachs were not used to it. We all became ill and Filip had developed typhoid. The British were terribly understaffed and unprepared to deal with the thousands of walking corpses they found. They were short-handed and couldn't help so many sick prisoners of war.

Liberation 3: Filip

Two days later I found my brother in a barrack behind the kitchen. He recognized me and looked up and said, "I want to be with you."

On his bed hung a notice, "To be evacuated to hospital, soonest possible." On Sunday, I spoke to the doctor in charge, asking him to move me to the same hospital. Sadly, that was not to be. I ended up in a different hospital, not knowing that that was the last time I would look into my brother's eyes in this life. After I was reunited with my mother and sister in Bergen-Belsen, we found out that Filip had been moved to the main hospital in Rotenburg which was in the British occupied zone.

When we arrived there we asked to see the patient list and a kindly nurse took out a list that was maybe 20 pages long.

We found his name but also found out that he had died on May 19th. I was heartbroken, and I could see that my normally strong mother was crumbling, like her spirit was leaving her body. We managed to hang on and support each other as they led us to a mass grave where he was buried. They said we were welcome to place a Star of David on one of the graves to symbolically mark the place of a Jewish person. They were very sympathetic people and I will never forget their kindness in our hour of grief. It seems strange to think that none of them are alive today that they, too, like the patients they treated have passed on.

My mother was being brave, but I could see that she was breathing deeply to stabilize herself and keep the grief from taking over. I kept telling her that at least we are three people who survived. We must be grateful for that. We have to make the best out of this. We cannot bring Filip back. We stayed there, at the hospital, for two days in a guest room made available for people in similar situations.

Hospital staff tried to console us by telling us that life must go on saying, "You are fortunate to have so many left in your family." We returned to the camp and my mother stayed on there.

My mother gradually regained her strength and made peace with Filip's death. We all had to go on with our lives.

Hatred can do more harm to you than all of the things that other people do to you. No person can go back to living normally with a feeling of ever-present hatred in his heart. One must reconcile with the past. I prayed and thanked God for my blessings, especially the blessing of survival, for finding my mother and sister and for the years I was able to spend with Filip. May he rest in peace.

I made a little sketch of the cemetery on the hospital grounds with all the unmarked mass graves of the victims. I look at it today and know that Filip's life has touched me in ways I can never fully describe. I know he knows that, and that is enough.

My drawing of the mass graveyard at Main Rotenburg Hospital May 19, 1945

CHAPTER 6

Rebuilding:
Putting the pieces back together

I stayed on in Bergen-Belsen along with thousands of others. We stayed there because there was decent housing and safety for all of us. As I said earlier, the authorities kept the gas chambers and crematorium intact as proof to the Germans of the horrible atrocities that were committed on these grounds. Later, they decided to level them.

Our barrack was within walking distance to the crematorium. There must have been at least a hundred barracks altogether. The British brought many survivors from the area to Bergen-Belsen because of its infrastructure (many of the barracks had been built originally to house German soldiers who worked at the camp). Because of our liberation and the feeling that in some strange way we were on ground that was consecrated by the deaths of our friends, we were able to push away the eeriness of the place and make this camp of death a place of rebirth.

The past was gradually receding, replaced with the promise of a possible future for those of us who wished to grab it. Many former prisoners were unable to make the transition, however, and retreated deep into themselves. Reaching them took a long time, but the doctors did not give up.

I ended up staying at Bergen-Belsen for three whole years before eventually emigrating to the United States. During that three-year period I met my future wife, Judy, may she rest in peace, and she helped me learn how to live again. Who would have thought that from the roots of this evil place, a place that is now synonymous with torture and pain that a garden of hope could grow!

Certainly not me. I had to experience it for myself to believe it was possible. Judy and I were married in a simple ceremony in the camp. She wore a wedding dress that had been passed from bride to bride. I like the symbolism of that.

Each new life leaves remnants of itself behind for others to pick up. In this case, the dress passed on hope to each new woman who wore it. It is perhaps symbolic of a greater lesson, that life is never complete without love.

Soon, Judy got pregnant and we left for America. My son, Filip was born shortly after our arrival in New York which was on the 22nd of June 1950. After staying a month with relatives there, we moved to Boston. We had another child, a beautiful daughter we named Susan, and later we all settled in Lowell, Massachusetts before Judy and I moved to Albuquerque in 1979.

Judy's story

Judy was born in 1929 and was only ten when the Germans invaded Poland. She was an only child and lived with her divorced mother in Lodz. The Germans marched into Lodz on a Friday and the next morning the inhabitants of the buildings were told by loudspeaker to assemble in one of the town squares. The schools were closed and so were the businesses, so Judy's family survived on what was left in their larder.

Three months later, and in the middle of the night, the Germans knocked on the door of their apartment building and told all the occupants they had ten minutes to gather their belongings. Judy told me that her mother was hurriedly emptying out her bureau drawers into a sheet. When all were assembled on the street they were put in streetcars and taken to large factory buildings.

Early the next morning, the Germans let all the non-Jews free and forced the Jews into cattle cars. The train started up and for 3-4 days they journeyed to an unknown destination without food or water. Judy's family, that included her mother, grandmother, an aunt and a cousin, were then let out of the cattle car and re-housed in an empty synagogue.

They struggled mightily through the harsh winter, trading articles of their clothing for food from nearby farmers. By March there was nothing left to trade and Judy's mother hired a Polish smuggler to spirit them back to Lodz where the plan was to re-enter their apartment and recover some more of their possessions.

Judy's mother gave the smuggler all their money and her jewelry for railroad tickets and false papers because it was forbidden for Jews to travel. They were on the road for one month masquerading as non-Jews and finally managed to get back to Lodz and their apartment only to find other people living there!

Their plan had failed. It was impossible to get their things. Meanwhile, the Germans had begun to erect barbed wire fences, and in just a matter of a few short days the ghetto was up and running. Unable to escape, they spent the next four years struggling to survive the ghetto life. They never found out what had become of their relatives who had been left behind in eastern Poland.

Judy was given the job of embroidering insignia on German uniforms and for her efforts was given a bowl of soup at work. Her mother would meet her on the way home and Judy shared her soup with her. It was the only food they had.

They remained in the ghetto until 1944 and managed, somehow, to evade the many random *selections* for the concentration camps. Little by little people were sent away. The Germans said they were being sent to work camps, but Judy's family knew better.

The winters, especially the winter of 1944, were hard. They had no heat or proper clothing. Bodies were piling up in the streets. Because people were starving and because the Germans promised them work in camps, some felt they would be better off going rather than freezing to death.

To add insult to injury, the Germans forced people in the camps to write letters home saying that the work was hard but that there was plenty of food and good conditions and that others (Jews) shouldn't be afraid to go to the camps. Few relatives, if any, believed the letters.

Escape from the ghetto was nearly impossible as German soldiers were stationed every hundred feet or so. To hear Judy tell it, "After four years of starving and freezing we knew the end was near. The *selections* came more frequently, on a daily basis." Judy and her mother hid briefly in a room sealed off by a wardrobe closet, but they were without food or water. Finally, they decided it was their turn to go. The inevitable could not be postponed.

Selected, they were taken to Auschwitz during the night, and upon arriving they were told to undress and had their heads shaved. When they had arrived, there were several hundred people, but when they emerged there were only 50.

They were then made to sit down on the ground while a Jewish woman whose job it was to choose people for work details asked them where they were from. They told her and she asked if they knew a certain name. That name turned out to be Judy's mother's maiden name. As luck would have it, the woman turned out to be her cousin who had been living in France.

This woman was their salvation, for without that family connection, they would not have survived Auschwitz. At one point, Judy's mother was sent to the hospital and soon learned that Judy's whole barrack was being sent to the gas chamber. She then located the cousin who was able to smuggle Judy out. By the grace of God, Judy and her mother were soon transferred to Bergen-Belsen where they, like me, were eventually liberated but not before contracting typhoid and witnessing death on a large scale, up close.

Judy often remarked about the horrendous sight of mounds of bodies, stacked unceremoniously like wood in a pile. "Even for us," said Judy, "visualizing the piles of bodies was unbelievable. The horrors were indescribable."

I met Judy in 1946 and we fell in love. We were married three years later. I know that the memory of those years of imprisonment affected her life in ways normal people cannot imagine. It was good that we had each other and our shared experiences to see us through the 'black' times.

So strong and so vivid were the memories that she often wondered whether her life in America was real or not. She would occasionally live in two realities and would wake up from dreams thinking she was still in Auschwitz.

Judy would often quote Elie Weisel, an author who, himself, had survived the concentration camps: "It is easier to be in Auschwitz and imagine yourself free than it is to be free and imagine yourself in Auschwitz." Years ago, long before Judy's death, she visited the cousin in France she credits with saving her life. While in Europe, she also visited Germany. I remember she described that part of her trip like "walking barefoot on hot coals."

We had many wonderful years together, and I still see her face and can hear her voice in my head. She is gone now, but instead of mourning her death, I celebrate her remarkable life. It is the way she would have wanted it. May she rest in peace.

Maps and other items

List of items

Map of Free Poland 1920-1939

Map of Belarus with Smorgon after WWII

Map of Soviet-German Partition with Smorgon 1939

Modern day road map showing Smorgon

Modern day map of downtown Smorgon

Street map of Smorgon 1941

The Holocaust in Poland

Modern day map of Orany (Varena), Lithuania

Modern day map of Estonia

Modern day map of Ereda (Goldfield), Estonia

Modern day map of Neuengamme, Germany

Map of Neuengamme Concentration Camp 1942-45

Map of Stutthof Concentration Camp, Fall 1944

Photo of prisoners' rail car at Stutthof

Photo of prisoners' barracks at Stutthof

My certificate from the British Zone

Poem: The loss of my father (Aron Straser)

Poem: To meet my father (Judy Straser)

Poem: The deluge (from the original in Yiddish)

Poem: A mountain of shoes (Aron Straser)

Poem: Smorgonie (Aron Straser)

Map of Free Poland 1920-1939

Courtesy of State University of New York at Buffalo

Map labels:

SWEDEN

LATVIA

Baltic Sea

Free City
of Danzig
(Gdańsk)

LITHUANIA

Wilno
(Vilnius)

SOVIET
UNION

GERMANY

Minsk

POMERANIA

MASURIA

Stettin
(Szczecin)

Białystok

Berlin

Warsaw

GERMANY

Łódź

Breslau
(Wrocław)

Lublin

Kiev

UPPER
SILESIA

Prague

Kraków

Gorlice

EASTERN
GALICIA

SOVIET
UNION
(1922-39)

CZECHOSLOVAKIA

AUSTRIA

HUNGARY

ROMANIA

N

Legend:

- - . - International boundary
—— Boundary of Poland established 1921
National capital
Populated place
LATVIA Country or region

From Soviet Russia
From Austria
From Germany
Determined by plebiscites, 1920-21
Annexed from Czechoslovakia, 1938

0   75   150 Kilometers
0   75   150 Miles

Map of Belarus with Smorgon after World War II

Map courtesy of Magellan Geographix

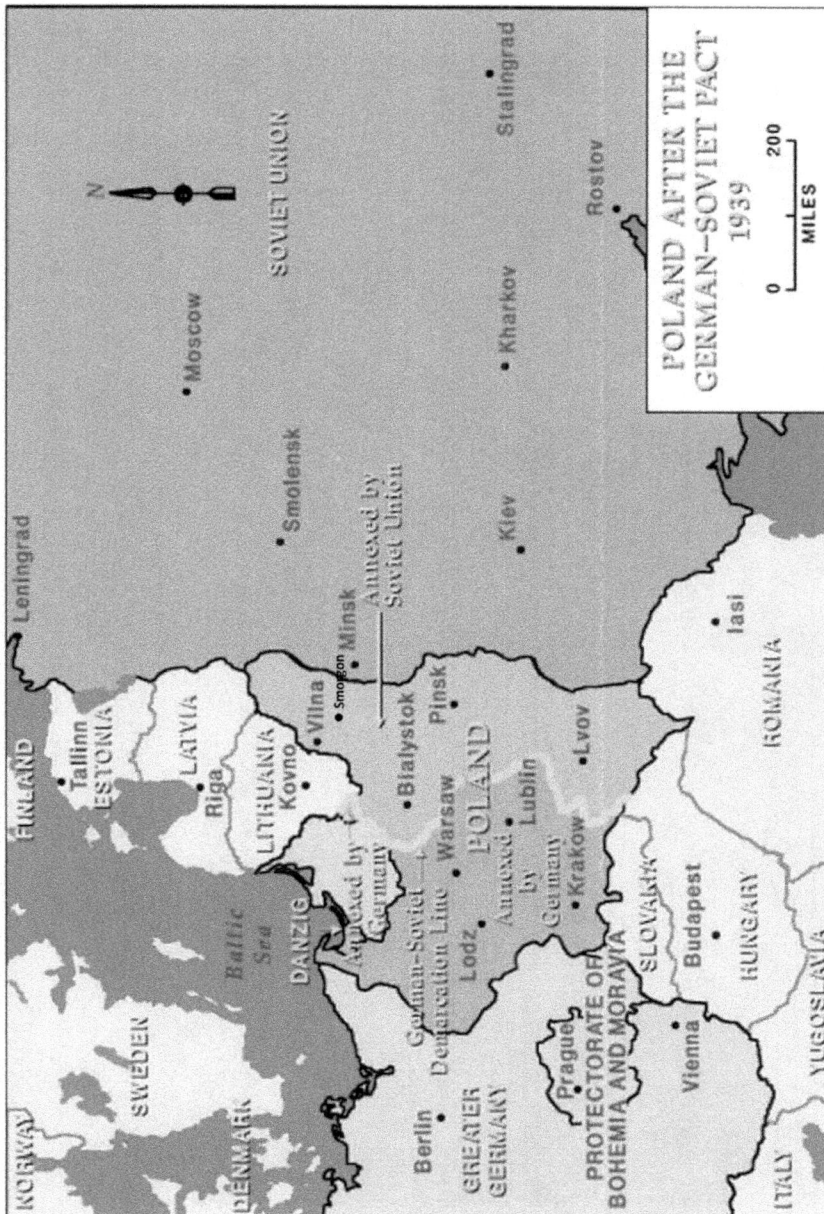

Map of Soviet-German Partition 1939 with Smorgon
— *US Holocaust Memorial Museum*

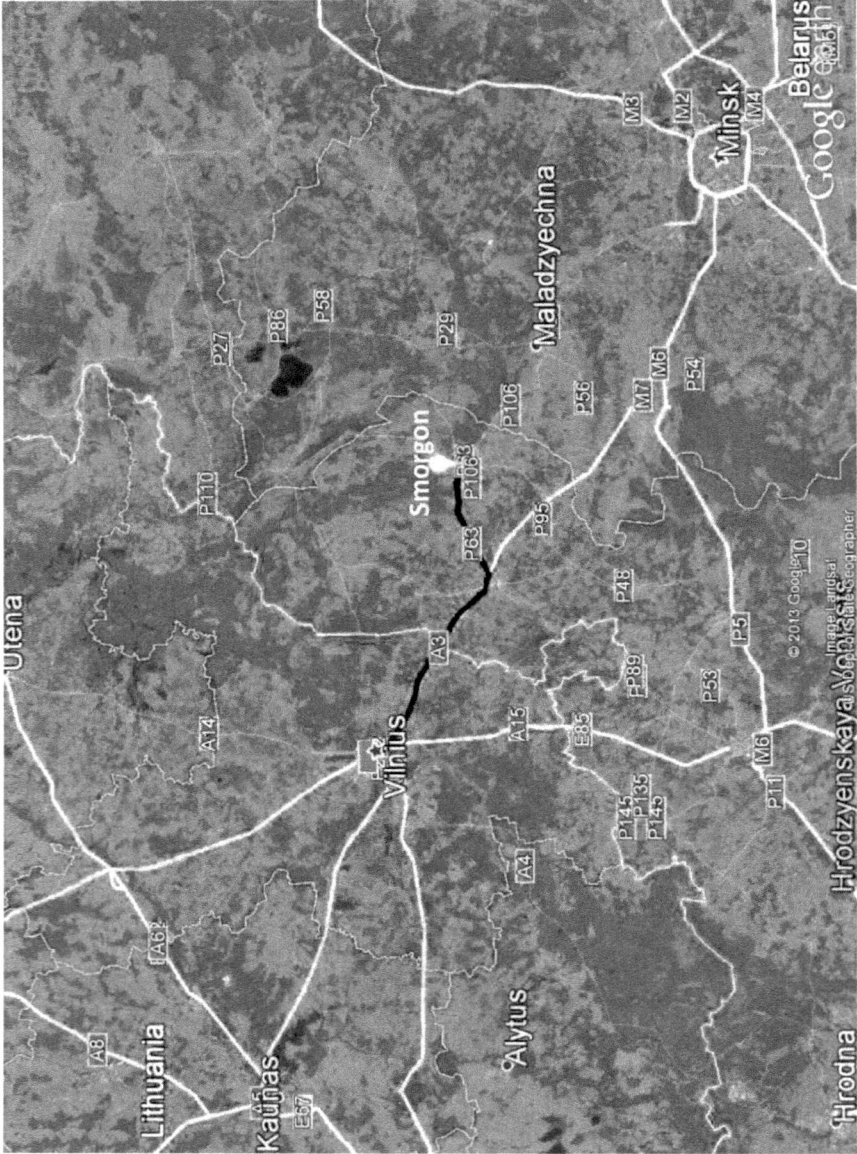

Modern day road map showing Smorgon
Courtesy of Google Maps

Modern day map of downtown Smorgon
Courtesy Google Maps

מפת העיר סמורגון

Map of the City of Smorgon

הוכן ע"י : אליעזר קרפל, מרדכי טבוריסקי. ישראל לוינסון.

Elyezer Karpel, Mordechay Tabourisk & Israel Levinson

Street map of Smorgon 1941

The Holocaust in Poland

⚇ Extermination camp
⚈ Main city with ghetto
■ Major concentration camp

LITHUANIA
(1 Sep 39)

Wilno

Ponary ⚇ ⚈

Reichs-
kommissariat
Ostland (Dec 41)

Stutthof ■
Reichsgau
Danzig-Westpreußen ■ Soldau

Provinz
Ostpreußen

Potulice ■ Bydgoszcz ⚈ ⚇

Chełmno ⚇

Reichsgau
Wartheland
(POLAND)

Treblinka ⚇
Ciechanów ⚈
⚈ Warsaw ⚇

Sieradz ⚈ ⚈

Łódź ⚈

Radom ⚈

⚈ Kielce Lublin

Provinz
Nieder-
schlesien ■

Gross-
Rosen

Provinz
Oberschlesien

Będzin ⚈

Majdanek ⚇

Kraków ⚈ ⚇
■ Płaszów

Auschwitz-Birkenau

Zasław ■

Białystok ⚈ Nowogródek ⚈ ⚇

Bezirk Białystok
(22 Jul 41)

⚈ Brześć

Sobibór ⚇

Reichs-
kommissariat
Ukraine (1 Sep 41)

Kowel ⚈

Generalgouvernment ⚇
(POLAND) Bełżec

⚈ Łuck
⚇ Polanka

Lwów ⚈

Tarnopol ⚈

CZECHOSLOVAKIA

Distrikt Galizien
(1 Aug 41)
⚈

Stanisławów ⚈

Map showing Orany (Varena), Lithuania
Courtesy Google Maps

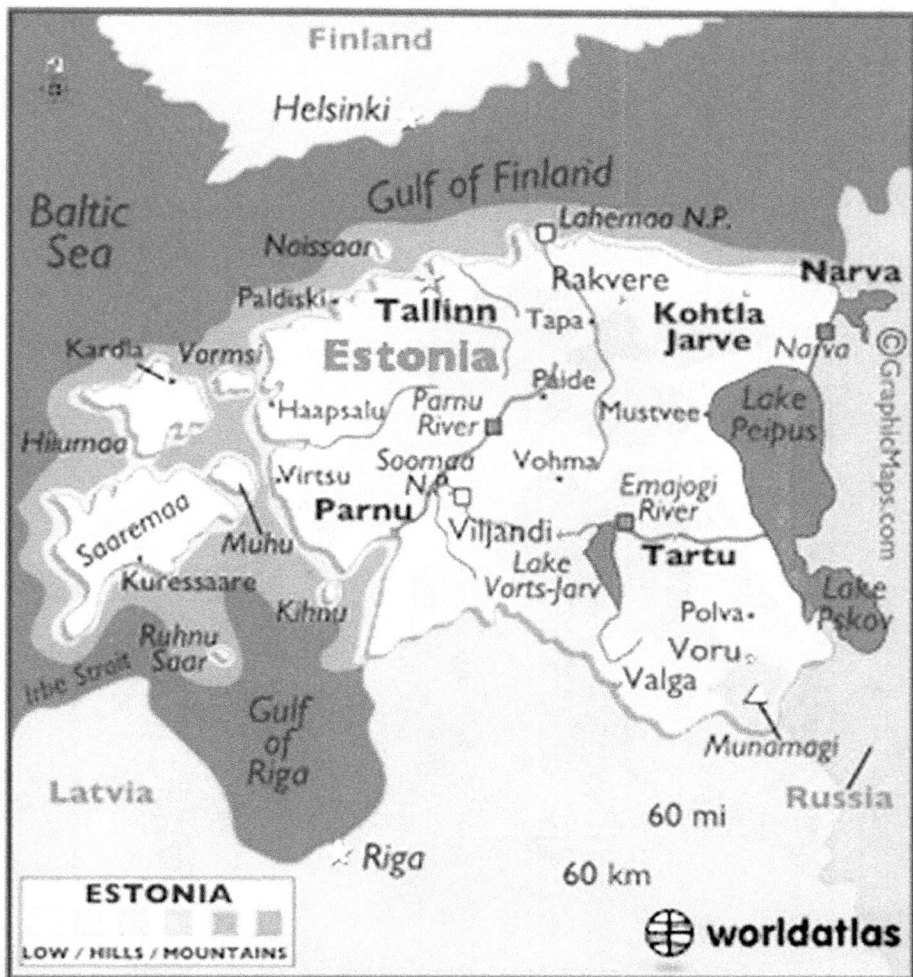

Modern day map of Estonia
Courtesy Worldatlas

Modern day map of Ereda (Goldfield), Estonia
Courtesy Google Maps

Modern day map of Neuengamme, Germany
Courtesy of Google Maps

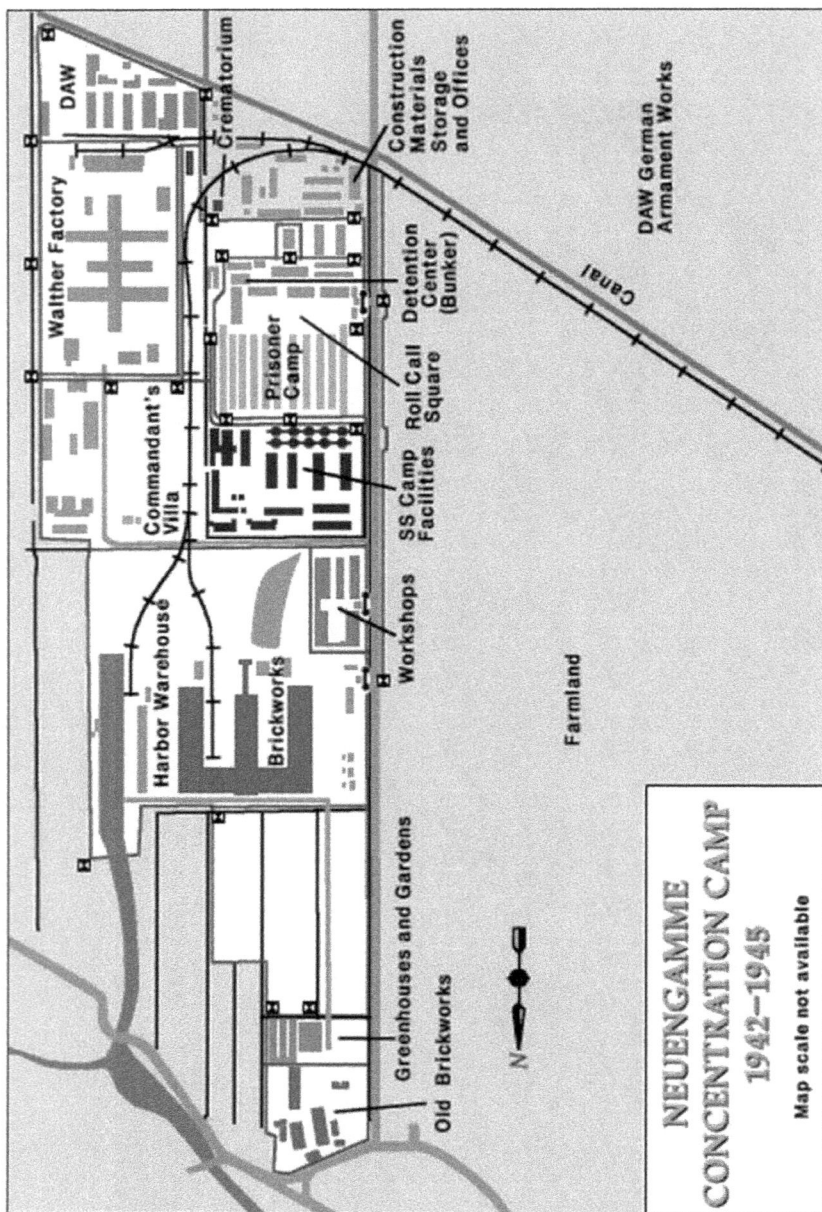

Neuengamme Concentration Camp 1942-1945
— US Holocaust Memorial Museum

DAW

Crematorium

Walther Factory

Construction Materials Storage and Offices

DAW German Armament Works

Canal

Detention Center (Bunker)

Prisoner Camp

Roll Call Square

Commandant's Villa

SS Camp Facilities

Workshops

Harbor Warehouse

Brickworks

Farmland

Greenhouses and Gardens

Old Brickworks

NEUENGAMME CONCENTRATION CAMP
1942–1945

Map scale not available

N

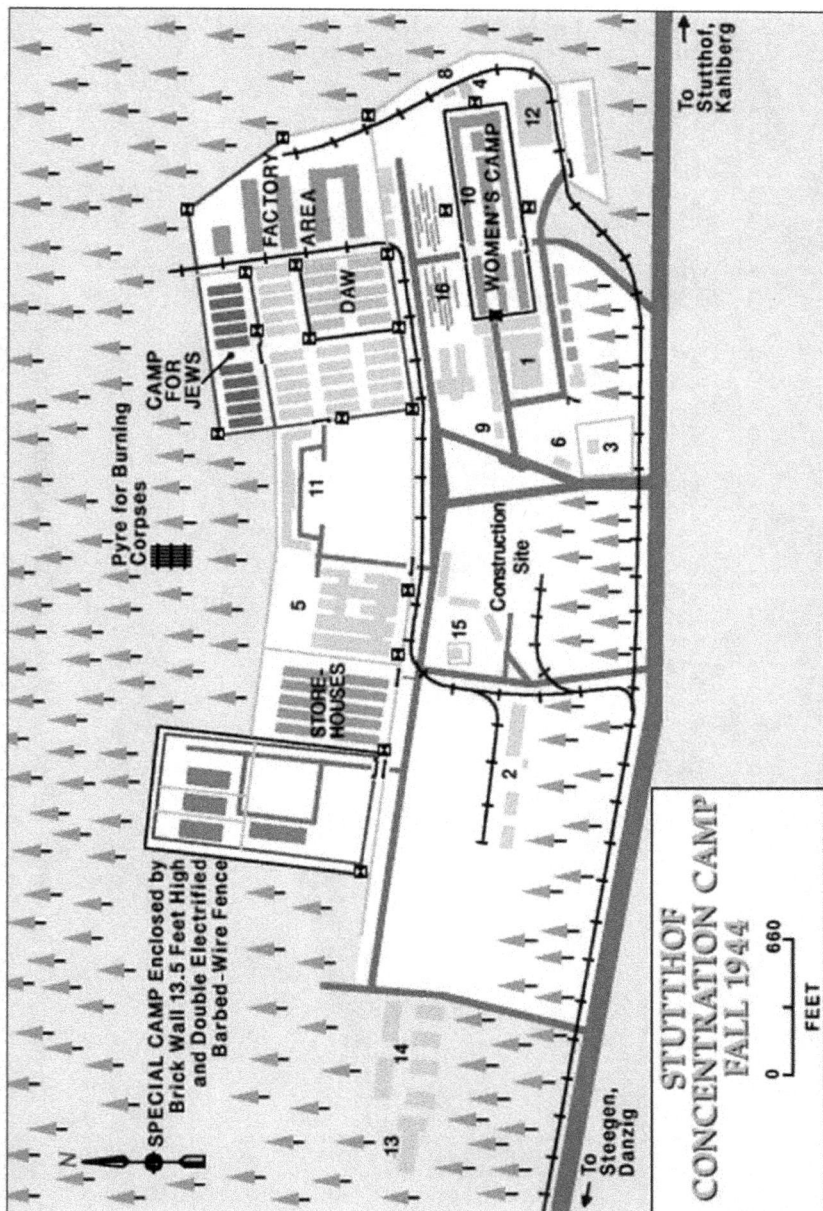

Stutthof Concentration Camp Fall 1944
– *US Holocaust Memorial Museum*

Map labels:

N

SPECIAL CAMP Enclosed by Brick Wall 13.5 Feet High and Double Electrified Barbed-Wire Fence

Pyre for Burning Corpses

CAMP FOR JEWS

FACTORY AREA

DAW

WOMEN'S CAMP

Construction Site

STORE-HOUSES

To Stutthof, Kahlberg

To Steegen, Danzig

STUTTHOF CONCENTRATION CAMP FALL 1944

0   660

FEET

13   14   11   5   2   15   9   6   3   1   10   16   12   4   8   7

Prisoners' rail car outside Stutthof Concentration Camp

Stutthof Concentration Camp Barracks

My certificate from the British zone

The Loss Of My Father
by Aron Straser

The war had just begun, full of hunger and horror
Food getting scarce, by the day, by the hour.
My father left early saying "will be back tomorrow"
And that was the last time I said "bye" to my father.

The meager belongings, to trade for some flour
My father took with him, to the nearest farmer.
He is late! Every minute drags on like an hour.
He did not return. Where are you now, Father?

The night an eternity, and we are so helpless
Impatiently waiting for dawn to break, my mother.
"Take care of yourselves" Mom could hardly express,
"I must go out and look for your father."

The door slowly opened, in the dimly lit room
A spasmodic sobbing reached our ears.
While making an effort to conceal her gloom
Her body was trembling, her eyes full of fear.

Then embracing my sister, myself and my brother
I could taste the salty tears on her face.
Oh how she aged! my grief-stricken mother
Bewildered, heartbroken, as if in a daze.

She hugged us tightly, to make us feel safer
As if to minimize what she dreaded to say.
To utter the words, mother couldn't master
We knew without saying - We are orphans today!

Mother took a sip of cold water to swallow
To moisten her lips, and to soften her thirst.
"I feel so empty, frightened and hollow
G-D help us!" she cried, in a prayer of hers.

We stood in a circle, and cried there forlorn
And promised to care for, and help one another.
Like lost little birds, in the eye of a storm
Oh how we need you and miss you now, Father!

Somewhere in Poland, in a place unknown
In a mass grave lie the remains of my father.
Rest In Peace, dear beloved, your soul in heaven
We will always remember you, love you and mourn!

To Meet My Father
by Judy Straser

The long-awaited hour, here!
I fly to meet my father
Impatient days all tallied now
Fly faster on, fly faster.

For my father is awaiting me
And as my heart is racing
My journey's almost over now
The miles are erasing.

And every part of me awakes
The joy this moment means
Mere words alone cannot express
What's real, and not just dreams.

My tired eyes begin to close
I'm lulled by engines humming
The past invites me to its cave
For memories awakening.

And now I'm back to ages past
My gaze to you lifts higher
I want you to belong to me
And show you off as Father.

I'm a mother. Will you know me now?
When life's uproar pulled us apart
I know for sure one thing alone
We share one soul, one heart.

Why?

Who can make the answer sound?
You cannot: fated to never know
Our Creator's ways confound.

You, mentsch, are truly blessed
World rulers and angels' peer
You who put your minds to the test!

Your limits are set
And dead-ends frustrate inquiry's quest
And you'll never find out
You'll only regret.

The souls who perished
Demand to know:
Were our sins so over-powering
To be punished with the pain of Hell?

Survivors' trembling hours
Confronting not-human fates
Sorrowing
Choking
Coming from the innermost places

What is my purpose? To what end?
Why was I worthy to survive?
Questions, not answers
Torture my brain
In these sleepless nights.

The Deluge
by Aron Straser 1994

Neuengamme, Aurich, Meppen
– the names come to mind.

The Allied forces are getting ready
to open the invasion of Europe
to crush the military might of Germany.
Even Mother Nature was merciless.
They moved us here, to dig anti-tank trenches
around the cities of Aurich and Meppen.

Black, thick clouds cover the skies.
The sun has been hiding for a week or more.
On the ground, wet creatures like ghosts
cling to each other in pain and despair.

We return to the barracks, tired and hungry.
The tasteless quart of soup our reward for the day.
Our wet clothes strung up above our straw sacks,
The wet drops, like tears fall on our faces.
On the straw sack next to me, the body of my brother.
Something is pressing my chest, full of pain.
My extremely tired body is aching for rest.
The night is short. The siren will surely shriek again.

A Mountain of Shoes
by Aron Straser

The mountain is tall, shapeless and ugly
The mountain is gruesome
What a horrible sight
A giant waste pile of personal remnants
The mountain is several stories high.

I saw the "shoe" mountain
In the camp of Stuthoff
Not far from the Chimney
Of the huge crematorium
This awful pile of human footwear
Carried a message, a message of doom.

Many lives are snuffed out here in Stuthoff
Transports of victims arrive every day
The angel of death, dressed like a Nazi
Feeds the flames in the ovens
The smoke from the chimney
is heavy and gray.

Hundreds of thousands of shoes are
Ripped open, examined for valuables
Searched for loot
Then thrown on top of the ugly mountain
The mountain grows bigger and cries to heaven
But no one hears! The world is blind, deaf and mute.

There is no computer designed as yet
To store the volume of data one would get
From the stories of agony, sacrifices and bravery
Of barbarism, inhumanity and earthly hell
If only the remnants the only witnesses
If only the shoes, could speak and tell.

Smorgonie
by Aron Straser

On the banks of the Vileya River in Poland,
In the state of Vilna,
You can find the small community
Where my mother used to rock me in my cradle
In the village of Smorgon.

I recall a summer day on Sabbath,
Jewish families would meet in Sinietski's Park.
The youthful years bring back
Countless memories of Smorgon that was.

Wednesday is a market day in town.
Farmers, peasants, packed the square.
Yiddish and White Russian babble mix.
So outstanding, so unique,
But you don't hear their Yiddish anymore.
It is gone with the Jews forever.
From Smorgon that once was.

In Poland where Jewish culture flourished,
Contributed a lot to the moral fiber of the state,
They will be remembered as a good people,
God-fearing, peace-loving.
Shalom, Shalom, Shalom.

Postscript

There were many who took revenge on the German guards. In some cases it was illegal. I was taught that a man, any man, must be responsible for his actions.

However, in those times when a man's life could hang by a thread and be decided capriciously by a guard's bad mood, it is difficult to condemn the actions of those who took retribution against their captors. While I understand their motivation and justification, my faith tells me that to murder a murderer without a trial would make me no better than the man I would kill.

I am convinced that many of the German people - not all of them - were kept in the dark about the camps and the atrocities that were committed there in the name of the German Fatherland. How else could any human being live with that knowledge and go about his business while millions were being slaughtered? I know I could not.

As for today's Germans, how can any of us blame successive generations for the crimes committed by parents or now, grandparents?

Nonetheless, we know now that many young Germans bear an enormous silent guilt for their country's former leaders' attempts to exterminate the Jewish people. They know, too, that the atrocities of the Nazi Third Reich, will forever be a black mark on their history - and that they must live with it. While there are some who encourage the Jewish community to *get over it* and to *put it all behind us*, we cannot and, indeed, should not.

Were we to do so, we would dishonor the millions of people who suffered and died at the hands of evil men who followed an evil ideology.

If those deeds were left to gather dust on the pages of unopened history books they would not serve to remind us that the only way for evil to triumph over good is for good men and women to do nothing...or remember nothing.

Many of the freed Jewish prisoners went to Israel to work on the Kibbutz. I chose not to, though I did think about it. Neither did I end up refusing my restitution from the German government for my imprisonment. To have rejected it would have harmed my wife, my soon-to-be-born son and later, daughter. I came to the conclusion that I would not be punishing my former oppressors by refusing it; I would be punishing the future of my family.

While reparations cannot bring back the dead, they can, at least, help the living...and I was alive! Had I taken revenge against my guards I would still be in prison, not in a physical prison mind you, but a prison of the soul where I could never receive absolution for trying to justify the unjustifiable by committing the same brutality.

Hatred is destructive, not only for the victim, but also for its purveyor. It is an insidious emotion, working its way into the fiber of the soul, corrupting everything in its path. The temptation to hate can be strong and can arise from envy, jealousy, misinformation and peer pressure.

It can only be fought with wisdom and enlightenment. Fear and hatred feed off of each other, but neither one of them can thrive in an environment of truth and knowledge.

When we add forgiveness, tolerance and love to the mix, hatred hasn't even the slimmest chance of surviving. That is the lesson of the Holocaust and of my part in it. The Almighty saw fit to spare my life. Now I spend it praying that all men might have what I have...a life free of the bondage of hatred.

To borrow a phrase from the Sanskrit: "Today, well-lived, makes every yesterday a dream of happiness and every tomorrow a vision of hope."

Aron Straser

Aron (Struczanski) Straser was born on October 2, 1925 in Smorgon, Poland. He was just a teenager when the invading Nazi army swept through his village pushing his family out of their modest home in the small town of 10,000. He was captured and forced to work as a slave laborer, interred in several work and concentration camps in Lithuania, Poland, Estonia and Germany from June 30, 1941 until his liberation from the notorious death camp, Bergen-Belsen, in late April of 1945.

After marrying Judy, a young woman who was also a prisoner of Bergen-Belsen, on November 30th of 1948, they emigrated to the United States in 1949. They became parents to two children: a son, Filip and a daughter, Susan. The family lived for many years in Lowell, Massachusetts. After the children were grown, the couple moved to Albuquerque, New Mexico where Aron still lives today with his lovely wife of nine years, Miriam. He is an enthusiastic and accomplished wood-carver and an active member of his local temple where he raises his voice in song as its cantor on the high holy days.

About the Author

Stephan Helgesen is a retired U.S. diplomat who lived and worked in Europe, Asia, the Caribbean Basin and the Pacific Rim for over 25 years. He has authored four previous books and published over 250 articles in many local, national and international newspapers and periodicals. Since his retirement from the Foreign Service he has lived in the mountains outside Albuquerque, New Mexico. He is also the Honorary Consul for the Federal Republic of Germany in New Mexico.

"Meeting a survivor of the Holocaust is like touching a part of history that we'd like to forget but know we must remember. These witnesses of that horrible period are a living reminder to us that goodness doesn't exist in a vacuum and evil isn't restricted to the shadows. It was a humbling experience for me to interview Mr. Straser and a privilege to help tell his personal story to the world. There is only one word that can be added to this man's amazing journey to the light of freedom and it is, *shalom*."

www.ingramcontent.com/pod-product-compliance
Lightning Source LLC
Chambersburg PA
CBHW060950040426
42445CB00011B/1082